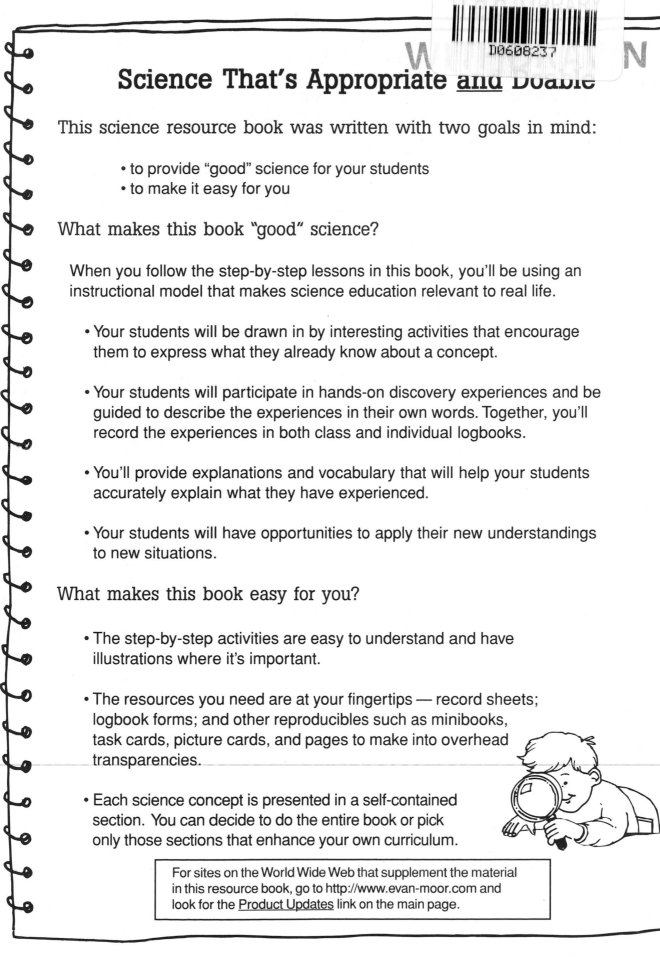

Science That's Appropriate and Doable

This science resource book was written with two goals in mind:

- to provide "good" science for your students
- to make it easy for you

What makes this book "good" science?

When you follow the step-by-step lessons in this book, you'll be using an instructional model that makes science education relevant to real life.

- Your students will be drawn in by interesting activities that encourage them to express what they already know about a concept.

- Your students will participate in hands-on discovery experiences and be guided to describe the experiences in their own words. Together, you'll record the experiences in both class and individual logbooks.

- You'll provide explanations and vocabulary that will help your students accurately explain what they have experienced.

- Your students will have opportunities to apply their new understandings to new situations.

What makes this book easy for you?

- The step-by-step activities are easy to understand and have illustrations where it's important.

- The resources you need are at your fingertips — record sheets; logbook forms; and other reproducibles such as minibooks, task cards, picture cards, and pages to make into overhead transparencies.

- Each science concept is presented in a self-contained section. You can decide to do the entire book or pick only those sections that enhance your own curriculum.

> For sites on the World Wide Web that supplement the material in this resource book, go to http://www.evan-moor.com and look for the Product Updates link on the main page.

Using Logbooks as Learning Tools

Logbooks are valuable learning tools for several reasons:
- Logbooks give students an opportunity to put what they are learning into their own words.
- Putting ideas into words is an important step in internalizing new information. Whether spoken or written, this experience allows students to synthesize their thinking.
- Explaining and describing experiences help students make connections between several concepts and ideas.
- Logbook entries allow the teacher to catch misunderstandings right away and then reteach.
- Logbooks are a useful reference for students and a record of what has been learned.

Two Types of Logbooks

The Class Logbook

A class logbook is completed by the teacher and the class together. The teacher records student experiences and helps students make sense of their observations. The class logbook is a working document. You will return to it often for a review of what has been learned. As new information is acquired, make additions and corrections to the logbook.

Individual Science Logbooks

Individual students process their own understanding of investigations by writing their own responses in their own logbooks. Two types of logbook pages are provided in this unit.

1. Open-ended logbook pages:
   Pages 4 and 5 provide two choices of pages that can be used to respond to activities in the unit. At times you may wish students to write in their own logbooks and then share their ideas as the class logbook entry is made. After the class logbook has been completed, allow students to revise and add information to their own logbooks. At other times you may wish students to copy the class logbook entry into their own logbooks.

2. Specific logbook pages:
   You will find record forms or activity sheets following many activities that can be added to each student's logbook.

At the conclusion of the unit, reproduce a copy of the logbook cover on page 3 for each student. Students can then organize both types of pages and staple them with the cover.

Geology • EMC 857

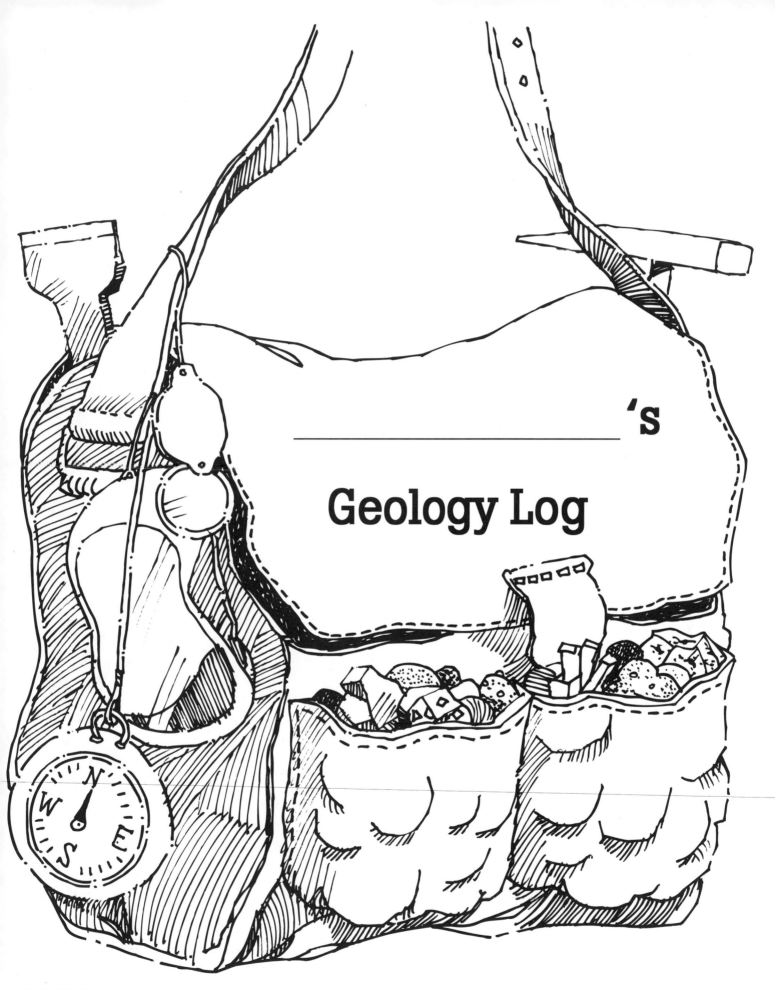

_____'s

Geology Log

Geology • EMC 857

Name _____

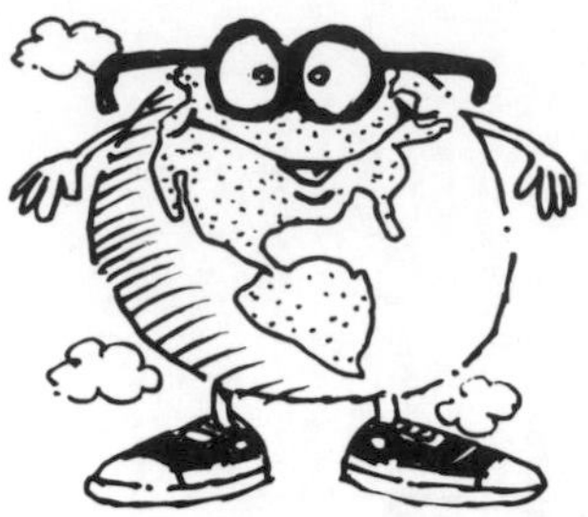

This is what I learned about geology today:

_____

_____

_____

_____

_____

_____

_____

_____

Note: Reproduce this form for students to record science investigations for their individual logs.

Name ____________________________________

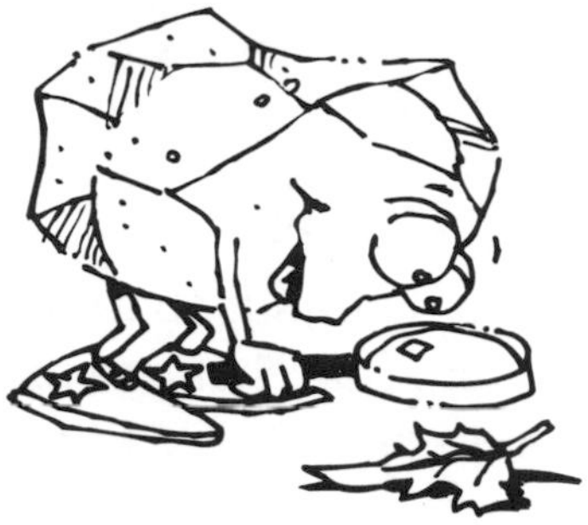

Investigation: ____________________________

What we did:

____

____

____

What we saw:

____

____

____

What we learned:

____

____

____

The Earth has layers— crust, mantle, core.

Locate the Layer

• Bring a peanut butter and jelly sandwich to class for this lesson. Say, "I am going to show you what is in my bag. I want you to describe it." Show them the sandwich and ask, "What do you see?" Ask them to describe the sandwich starting with the bottom layer. Continue asking, "What is the next layer?" until they reach the top slice of bread (*bread, peanut butter, jelly, bread*).

Then say, "Let's think about other things that have layers." Write students' ideas on the chalkboard and ask them to name the layers. For example:

birthday cake–cake, frosting, cake, frosting, candles
pizza–crust, sauce, pepperoni, cheese

• Divide the class into groups of three to explore layers. Each person in the group will explore one item (chocolate-covered cherry, sandwich cookie, or ½ of a piece of fruit). Students find and describe the layers their items contain and share that information with the other members in their group.

Materials for Each Group

• chocolate-covered cherry
• sandwich cookie
• 1/2 of a piece of fruit (a type containing one large seed)
• plastic knife (to cut open the chocolate-covered cherry)
• record sheet on page 11, reproduced for each student

Steps to Follow

1. Students separate their items into parts to examine the layers.
2. They identify and describe the layers on their record forms and write a definition of a layer.
3. Provide time for each group to share their findings with the rest of the class.

> *Layers*
> *A layer is one part of something laid on another part.*
>
> *A cake has layers.*

Follow Up

Begin a class geology log. Add the title "Layers" to a sheet of chart paper. Ask students to tell what they think a layer is. Write this on the chart paper. Explain that they have written a meaning for layers and that this meaning is called a definition. (You will return to the chart later to make corrections and additions.)

Gather Information

• Check your district audiovisual catalog for a filmstrip or video about the Earth's layers or read selections from books. Pages 27–29 of *The Magic School Bus, Inside the Earth* by Joanna Cole (Scholastic, 1987) and pages 1–15 from *Planet Earth/ Inside Outside* by Gail Gibbons (Morrow Junior Books, 1995) describe and illustrate the Earth's layers.

• Ask students to explain one way in which the piece of fruit and the Earth are alike (both have layers). Add a page entitled "Earth's Layers" to the class logbook. Have students write about the Earth's layers for their individual logs, using the form on page 4.

Earth's Layers
crust
mantle
outer core
inner core

A Trip to the Center of the Earth

After reading about the Earth's layers, complete the activity on page 12. Explain to students that they are going on an imaginary field trip to the center of the Earth.

Materials

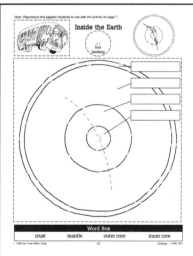

• pattern on page 12, reproduced on construction paper for each student
• paper fastener
• scissors
• crayons and pencil

Steps to Follow

1. Color the Earth's layers and the school bus.
2. Label the Earth's layers.
3. Cut out all the pieces along the dotted lines. Also cut the slit. (Younger students may need help with the slit.)
4. Fasten the bus and the backing together with the paper fastener.
5. Slip the backing behind the slit. Now the bus can move up and down the slit on its journey into the center of the Earth.

Follow Up

When the project is completed, have students work in pairs. Each student is to take a turn moving the field trip bus to the center of the Earth, naming each layer along the way.

Then call on a student to describe his or her trip to the center of the Earth, naming each layer. Ask more knowledgeable students to tell something about each layer after naming it.

Summary Activity

Reproduce the minibook on pages 13–15 for each student. They are to cut the pages apart, put the pages in order, and staple along the left side. Read the minibook together and confirm understanding of the information. Then have students complete the last two pages independently. (Note: Although we have not drilled into the mantle and core, geologists have figured out the Earth's structure by studying how earthquake waves move through the Earth.)

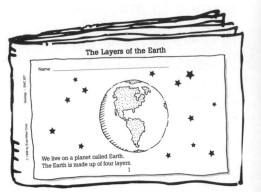

Extension Activities

Clay Models of the Earth

Materials

- small balls of clay—yellow, red, orange, blue, and green
- plastic knife
- record sheet on page 16, reproduced for each student

Steps to Follow

1. Have students roll a ball of red clay about 1" (2.5 cm) in diameter (the inner core).
2. Cover the red ball with a layer of yellow clay (the outer core). Try not to disturb the red layer.
3. Cover the yellow ball with a layer of orange clay (the mantle).
4. Cover the orange clay with a thin layer of blue clay and green clay (the crust). These represent the surface of the Earth covered with the blue water and green land.
5. Cut the model in half. (An adult will need to do this for younger students.)
6. Have each student name the layers of the model (crust, mantle, outer core, inner core) to a neighbor.
7. Complete the record sheet.

Geology • EMC 857

The Earth's Layers

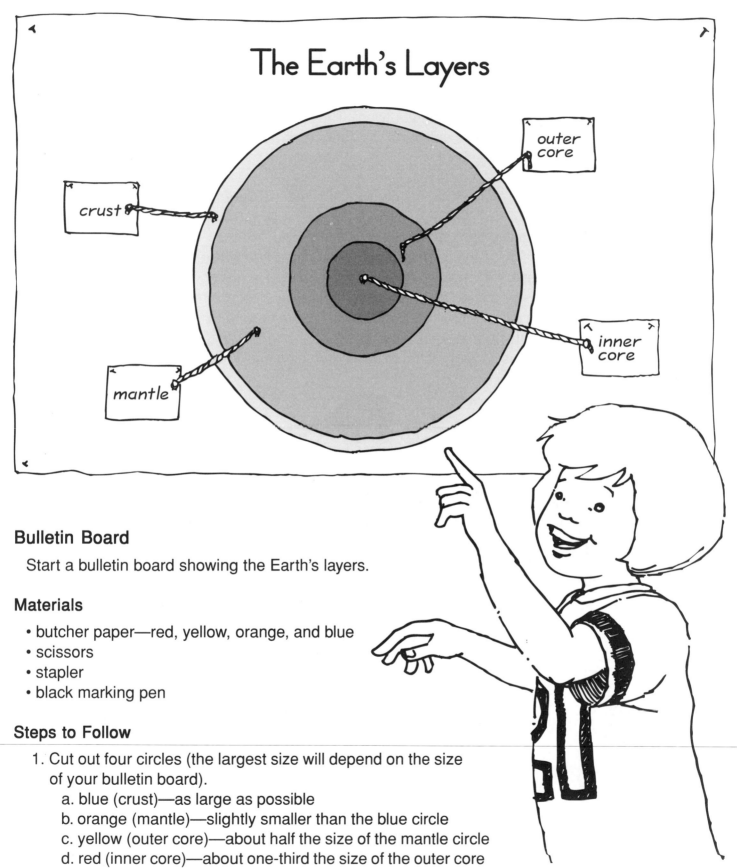

Bulletin Board

Start a bulletin board showing the Earth's layers.

Materials

- butcher paper—red, yellow, orange, and blue
- scissors
- stapler
- black marking pen

Steps to Follow

1. Cut out four circles (the largest size will depend on the size of your bulletin board).
   a. blue (crust)—as large as possible
   b. orange (mantle)—slightly smaller than the blue circle
   c. yellow (outer core)—about half the size of the mantle circle
   d. red (inner core)—about one-third the size of the outer core
2. Staple the layers on the bulletin board. Label each layer.

Geology • EMC 857

Earth Layers Chant

You will need a large area with plenty of room for students to move as they dramatize the Earth's layers.

1. Form a small circle of students facing outward. They represent the inner core of the Earth. Have a second row of students surround the "inner core" to represent the outer core.
2. Form a larger circle of students facing outward, around the "outer core" to represent the mantle.
3. Have seven children form a loose outside circle around the "mantle." They represent the plates of the crust.
4. Finally, assign each group of students a part of the chant.
    a. Students representing the outer and inner core stamp their feet and chant: *core, core, core.*
    b. Students representing the mantle put their hands out to support the crust, and rock from side to side as they chant: *mantle, mantle, mantle.*
    c. Students representing the plates of the crust move around the circle slowly and chant: *crust, crust, crust.*
5. Once each group knows its part, count to three, and have the "Earth" begin to move and chant.

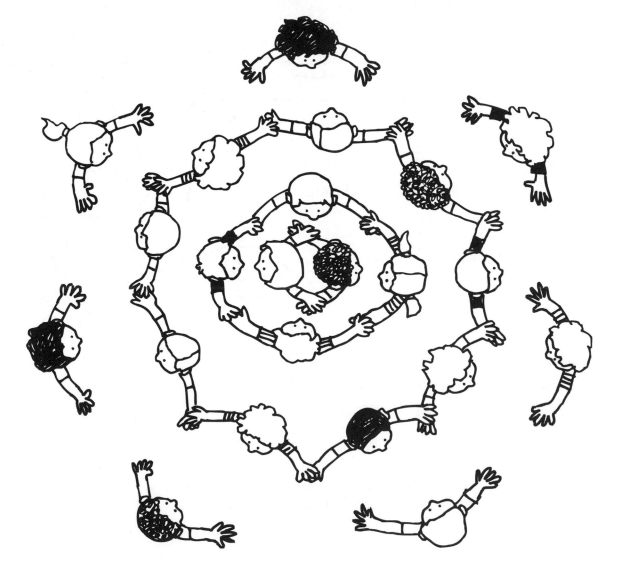

     Geology • EMC 857

Name _____

Layers

Label the layers.

chocolate-covered cherry

1. _____

2. _____

3. _____

sandwich cookie

1. _____

2. _____

3. _____

fruit

1. _____

2. _____

3. _____

A layer is

_____

_____

_____

_____

Inside the Earth

bus
backing

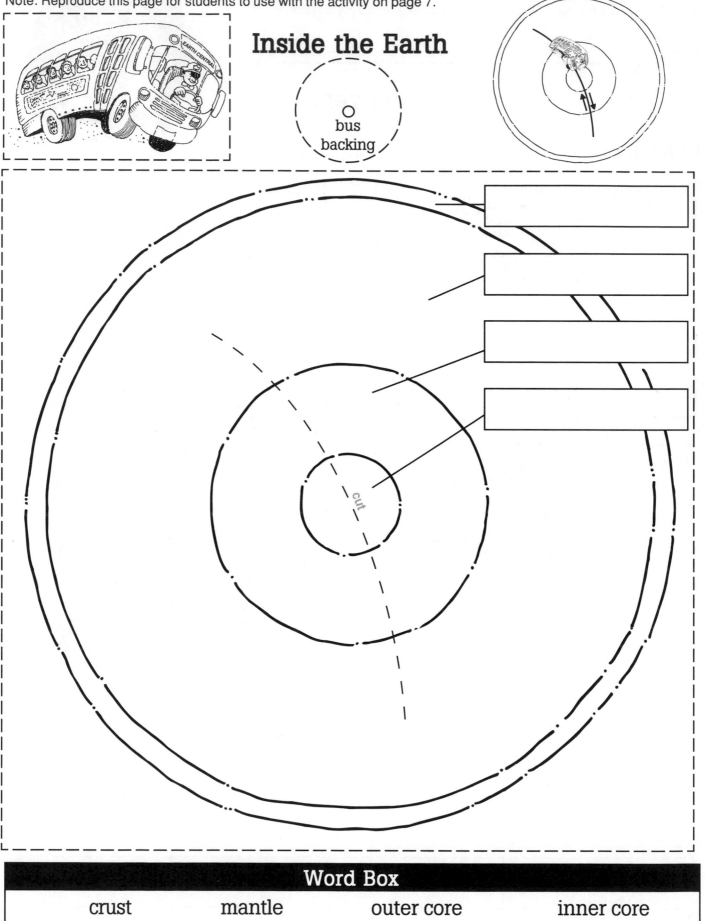

cut

Word Box			
crust	mantle	outer core	inner core

The Layers of the Earth

Name _____

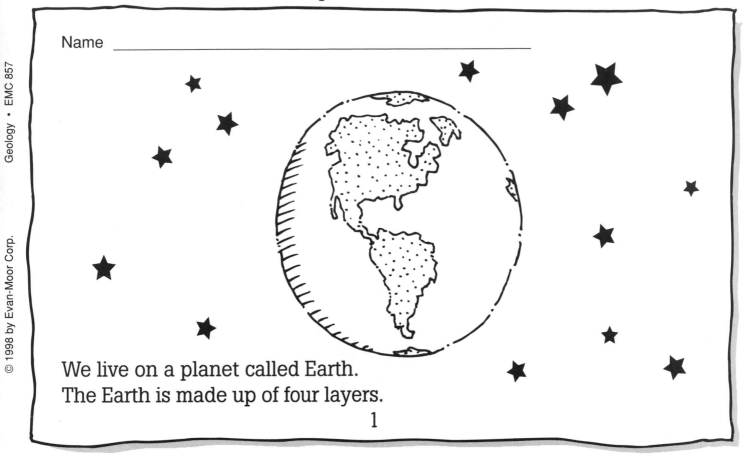

We live on a planet called Earth.
The Earth is made up of four layers.

1

The Crust

The outside layer of the Earth is called the **crust**. The crust is the part of the Earth you can see. It is the part of the Earth you can touch. It is the part of the Earth you walk on.

The crust is made up of rock and soil. It is very thin compared to the rest of the layers. In some places, it is only four miles thick.

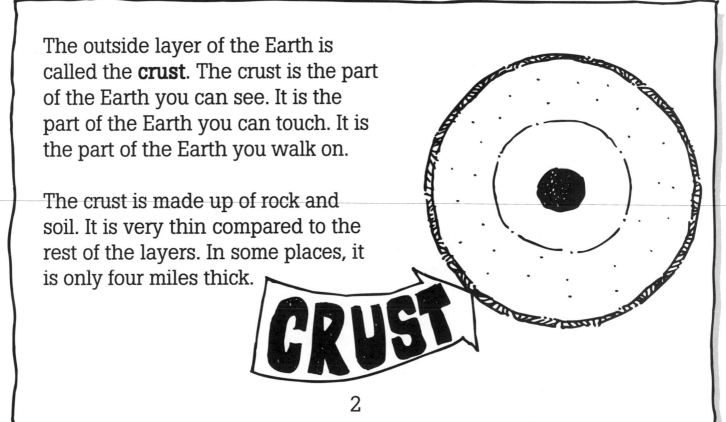

2

The Mantle

Under the crust is a layer called the **mantle**.

The mantle is made up of rocks and metals. Some of these rocks are so hot they are liquid. No one has gone down inside the mantle, but we have drilled into the top edge of it.

Sometimes the hot melted rocks in the mantle squirt up through cracks in the crust. This is called a volcano.

MANTLE

3

Geology • EMC 857

© 1998 by Evan-Moor Corp.

The Core

Under the mantle is the **core**. The core is the center of the earth.

The core has two parts. The **outer core** is so hot the rocks and minerals are liquid. The **inner core** is very, very hot also, but it is solid.

No one has ever been to the core. We cannot even drill that deep with our longest and strongest drills.

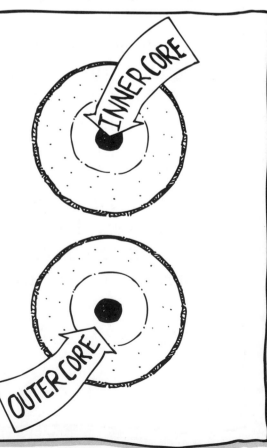

INNER CORE

OUTER CORE

4

Geology • EMC 857

© 1998 by Evan-Moor Corp.

Name the Layers

Here is a picture of the Earth cut in half.
Write the names of the layers on the lines.

5

Fill in the blanks.

| core | crust | mantle |

We walk on the Earth's _____.

The deepest part of the Earth is the _____.

The layer under the crust is the _____.

The coolest layer is the _____.

6

Name _____

The Earth's Layers

Color the crust green and blue.
Color the mantle orange.
Color the outer core yellow.
Color the inner core red.

The Earth's crust is made of rock and soil.

What Is on the Earth's Crust?

- Ask students to recall what the outside of the Earth is called. Explain that they are going to go outside to look at the "things" on the Earth's crust. Give each student a small lunch bag. Have them observe and collect samples of the things they find (soil, rocks, plant matter, dead insect parts, etc.).

- Back in class, provide time for students to share some of the items they collected. Then explain that the crust of the Earth is made of rocks and soil. Not everything found on top of the Earth is a part of the crust. Give several examples of what is and what isn't part of the crust using the items they collected.

pebble—"Yes, it is a rock and rocks are a part of the crust."

green leaf—"No. Only rocks and soil are part of the crust."

decayed leaf—"Yes. Dead leaves are part of soil and soil is a part of the crust."

- Have students separate their items into two categories — things that are part of the Earth's crust and things that are on the Earth's crust.

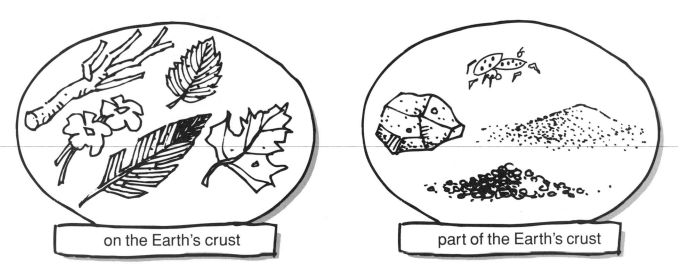

on the Earth's crust

part of the Earth's crust

Go through the items in each category asking, "Is this a part of the Earth's crust? Why (or why not)?" Make changes as needed, explaining why the item was in the incorrect category.

• Add a page entitled "The Earth's Crust" to the class logbook. Reproduce page 19 for students to record items that are either on or part of the crust for their individual logs.

Extension Activities

• Attach some of the items found to the "crust" of the Earth's Layers bulletin board (see page 9) with pins, tape, or glue.

• Take a field trip to an area where the Earth's crust has been cut (a mountain side, erosion along a river, etc.), so students can see the rock and soil of the crust cleared of surface matter.

• Reproduce the form on page 20 for each student. They are to draw and write about what they discovered on the field trip for their logs.

The Earth's Crust

The crust is the outside layer.

Soil is part of the crust.

Rocks are part of the crust.

Decayed plants and animals are part of the soil. That makes them part of the crust.

Geology • EMC 857

Note: Reproduce this page for students to use with the activity on page 18.

Name _____

The Earth's Crust

Draw what you found.

Circle the things that are part of the Earth's crust.

Name _____

Field Trip Report

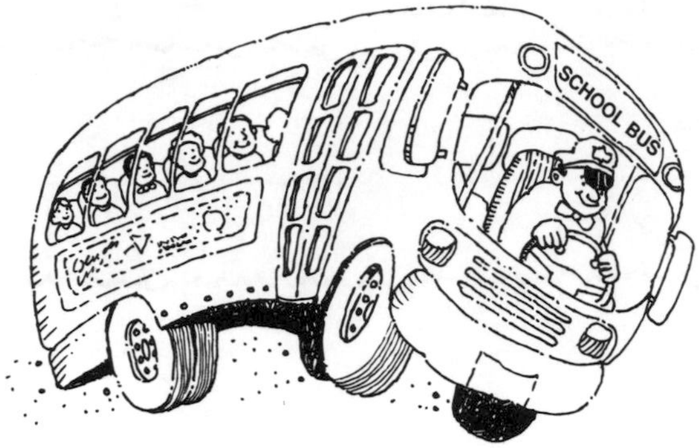

What I saw:

_____

_____

_____

_____

_____

What I learned:

_____

_____

_____

_____

_____

Soil is made when rocks break down and mix with decaying plants.

It's Not Just Dirt!

Bring in a soil sample. (Dig up the soil in a place where there is decaying plant matter.) Ask students to identify the sample and to describe what they see. Write their descriptions on a chart entitled "Things in Soil." Use page 4 for students to write in their individual logs.

Things in Soil
dirt
sand
gooey stuff
little rocks

A Closer Look at Soil

Divide the class into groups. Challenge students to discover what soil contains.

Materials

- newspaper
- wooden skewers (cut off sharp tips for younger students)
- soil sample
- sieve
- magnifying glass
- record form on page 24, reproduced for each student

Steps to Follow

1. Cover work areas with newspaper.
2. Students fill in the "What I think" portion of the record form.
3. Give each group a part of the soil sample.
4. Use the skewers to move particles around. Separate the soil into piles of similar particles. Use the magnifying glass to look closely at bits and pieces in the soil.
5. Use the sieve to separate sand from fine soil.
6. Students complete the "What I found" part of the record form.

Geology • EMC 857

Follow Up

- Provide time for groups to share their findings. Make corrections and additions to the class logbook (dead leaves, dead insects).

- Write the following questions on the chalkboard:
  "Are all soils the same?"
  "How are they alike?"
  "How are they different?"

  Pass around containers of different types of soils. Ask students to think about the questions as they examine (look at, feel, and smell) the soil. When everyone has explored the samples, call on students to answer the questions.

- Read appropriate pages from a book about soil, such as *Earth* by Alfred Leutscher (Dial Press, 1983) or *The Young Scientist Investigates Rocks and Soil* by Terry Jennings (Children's Press, 1982) to verify what soil contains. Prompt students to share what they learn from the story. Check the class logbook and individual logs to make corrections and additions.

- Reproduce a copy of page 25 for each student. Have them fold along the lines to create a minibook about soil to take home.

A Recipe for Soil

Now that students have developed an understanding of what soil contains, ask them to help write a "recipe" for making soil. Give each student a paper cup containing a sample of soil collected from under a tree. They are to examine it as the class works on the recipe. (This will help students recall what they discovered was in soil.)

1. List the "ingredients" good soil contains. (Review the contents of the soil minibook to confirm that everything needed has been listed.)
2. Develop steps to turn the raw ingredients into soil.
3. Reproduce page 26 and give one recipe card to each student. Make a copy of the recipe on a chart to go in the class logbook.

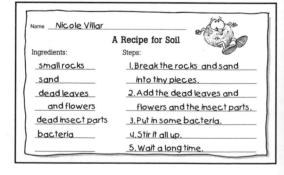

Extension Activities

Explore part of the process for creating soil using the following activities.

Make Sand

Materials

- lightweight rock (pumice, lava, or sandstone)
- hard stone
- magnifying glass
- safety goggles
- paper plate
- page 4, reproduced for each student

Steps to Follow

Let students take turns breaking rock into sand.
1. Put on the safety goggles.
2. Bang the lightweight rock against the hard rock to break off pieces.
3. Pick up the little pieces and put them on the paper plate.
4. Look at the pieces with a magnifying glass.

Follow Up

Have students describe what happened to the rock. *(The hard rock broke the lighter rock into little pieces.)* Ask, "What makes this happen in nature?" Guide students to the conclusion that wind and water move the rocks around causing them to bump against one another. Use page 4 for students to record what they learned for their individual logs.

Plants into Soil

Materials

- lunch waste (bread, banana peel, lettuce, etc., but no meat)
- a sign to mark the spot
- shovel
- page 5, reproduced for each student

Steps to Follow

1. Dig a hole in the soil about 1 foot (30.5 cm) deep. (Or fill a garbage pail with soil. Dig a hole in the center.)
2. Bury the wastes and mark the spot. Have the students write about what they did and what they think will happen.
3. Wait three months. Dig it up.
4. Discuss what is found.

Follow Up

Have students review what they wrote earlier. Ask them to describe how the food is different now. Ask them to explain how this is like what happens in nature to create soil. *(Plants and animals die, decay, and mix with tiny bits of rock to make soil.)* Have them complete their record forms.

Name _____

Soil

What I think soil contains:

_____

_____

_____

_____

What I found in the soil:

_____

_____

_____

_____

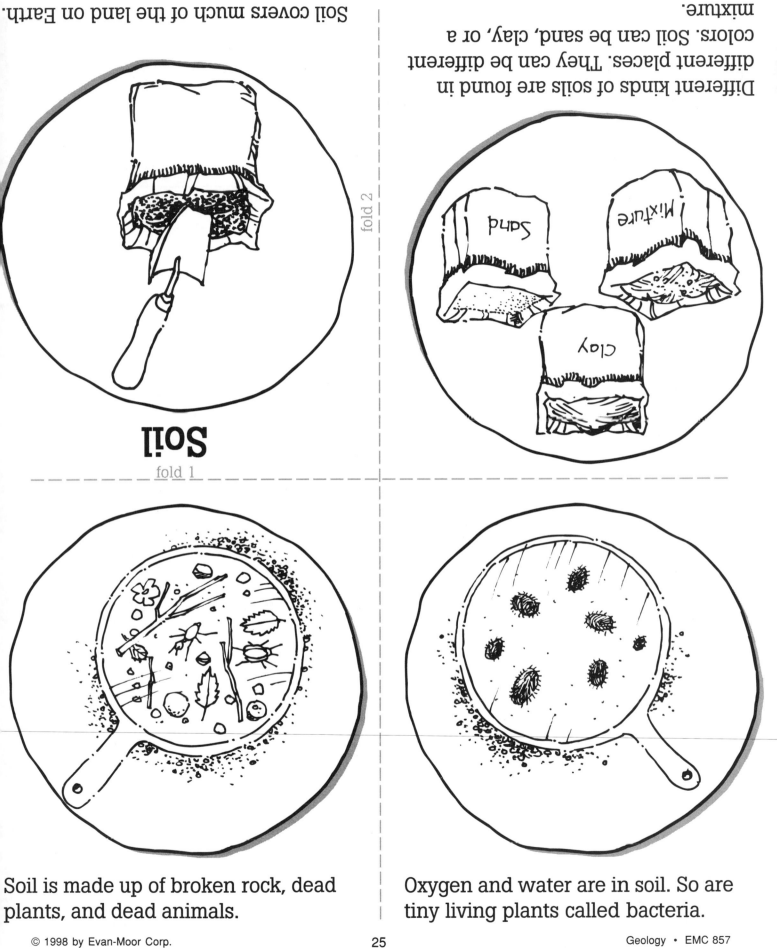

4

Different kinds of soils are found in different places. They can be different colors. Soil can be sand, clay, or a mixture.

1

Soil covers much of the land on Earth.

Soil

Soil is made up of broken rock, dead plants, and dead animals.

Oxygen and water are in soil. So are tiny living plants called bacteria.

Geology • EMC 857

2

3

Note: Reproduce this page for students to use with the activity on page 22.

Name ______________________________

A Recipe for Soil

Ingredients:

Steps:

Name ______________________________

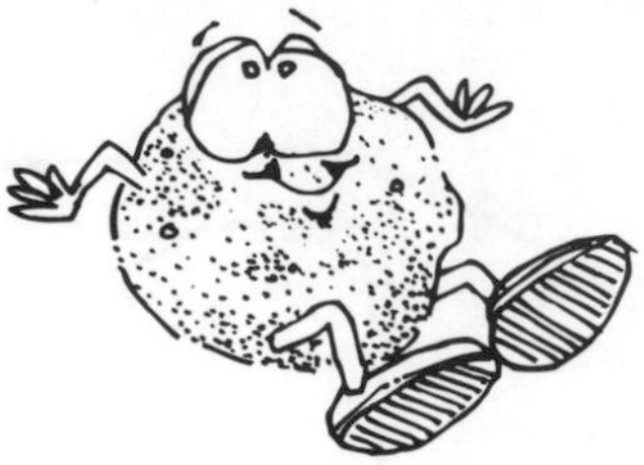

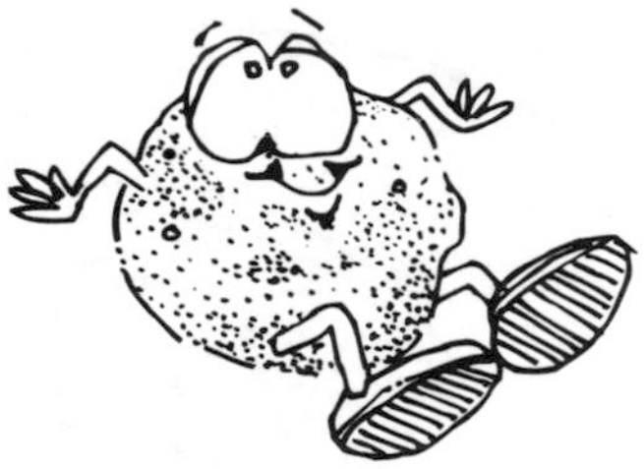

A Recipe for Soil

Ingredients:

Steps:

Rocks have different properties.

Before beginning this section, make sure your classroom rock collection has a variety of rocks. See the bottom of page 31 for a list of different types of rocks.

Rock Talk

Have students sit in a circle to talk about rocks.

1. Place a pile of rocks of various types in the center of the circle. (Include rocks of various sizes, colors, and textures.) Ask, "What can you tell me about these rocks?"
2. Record their comments in the class logbook on a page entitled "Rocks."
3. Pass around rocks for students to examine more closely. Ask them for words that describe the rocks. List words on a chart, and save it as a reference for writing experiences.

Rock Hounds

Take your young geologists on a rock hunt. The rocks collected will be used for investigations into rock properties.

> Rocks
>
> Rocks are hard.
>
> Some are big.
>
> Some are little.
>
> A rock can have spots.
>
> Most rocks are gray.

1. Give students paper bags for their collections. Emphasize that variety is more important than number. Explain that they are to collect only one of each type of rock they find. It's helpful to set a limit on the number of rocks collected, perhaps between five or ten per student.
2. Back in the classroom, read *Everybody Needs a Rock* by Byrd Baylor (Charles Scribner, 1974).
3. After the story, have students examine their rocks to select one to keep as their own. Reproduce pages 32–34 for each student. The students will use the pages to describe their special rocks. Encourage them to refer to the list of descriptive words created in "Rock Talk." Have students cut out the forms and staple them together to form individual books.

Put the rest of the rocks collected in a central location to use with the activities on pages 30 and 31. Depending on the kinds of rocks collected, you may need to add to the collection.

Sorting Rocks

Mark off sorting circles on the floor with two jump ropes. Have students think of ways to sort the rocks into two sets (large/small, light/dark, rough/smooth, solid color/many colors, shiny/dull).

Call on a student to make the two sets. (They don't need to use all the rocks every time.) After the rocks are laid in the circles, ask the student to explain why the division was made.

Rock Discovery Center

This center is not intended to be a structured activity. It is a time for students to discover rock properties on their own.

Materials

- classroom rock collection (include lava, pumice, and sandstone)
- balance scale
- large nail (for scratching rocks)
- string and scissors or measuring tape
- clear container and water
- paper towels

Steps to Follow

1. Set up an exploration center where students can measure, weigh, float, etc., rocks to discover more of their properties.
2. Demonstrate how the different equipment can be used.
3. Schedule times for small groups to take turns using the equipment.
4. When everyone has visited the exploration center, begin a page entitled "Rocks" for the class geology log.

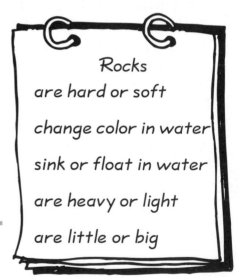

Rocks
are hard or soft
change color in water
sink or float in water
are heavy or light
are little or big

Rock Investigations

- With students assisting, do the explorations on pages 29 and 30 to validate their discoveries and correct any misconceptions about rocks. These exercises will allow students to explore the color, pattern, size, weight, hardness, and buoyancy of rocks.

- After completing the investigations, discuss with students any new information they have learned about rocks. Add this information to the class logbook page started earlier.

Colors and Patterns

Materials

- 6 to 10 rocks
- a clear container of water
- paper towels

Steps to Follow

Ask students to explain what they think is true about the colors and patterns of rocks. Then do this investigation to verify or correct their ideas.

1. Have students look at the rocks and determine what color each one is.
2. Place one rock at a time in the water. Observe any color changes.
3. Ask:
   a. What happens to the color of a rock when it becomes wet?
   b. Are all rocks only one color?
   c. Do patterns change when a rock becomes wet?
4. Record discoveries on a page entitled "Rock Properties" in the class logbook. Have each student use a copy of page 5 to record results in individual logs.

Size and Weight

Materials

- 6 to 10 rocks
- scissors
- ruler
- marking pen
- string
- balance scale
- masking tape

Steps to Follow

Circumference:
1. Select students to arrange the rocks in a row by size.
2. Stretch string around the middle of each rock. Cut the string. Use a ruler to measure the length. Explain that this number is how big around the rock is. Record the number on a piece of masking tape. Attach it to the rock. Repeat with each rock.
3. Make any changes to the order in which the rocks have been placed.

Weight:
Use the same set of rocks to determine weight.
1. Weigh each rock on the balance scale. (Use marbles in the other side of the balance.) Write the number of marbles the rock weighs on a piece of masking tape. Attach it to the rock.
2. Arrange the rocks from lightest to heaviest.

Follow Up

Ask:
   a. Can you tell which rock is the biggest around just by looking?
   b. Can you tell which rock is the heaviest just by looking?
Add discoveries in the class logbook page entitled "Rock Properties." Have each student use a copy of page 5 to record results in individual logs.

Hardness

While it is difficult to determine an exact scale for measuring hardness in the classroom, this investigation helps students understand that there are variations in hardness among different types of rocks.

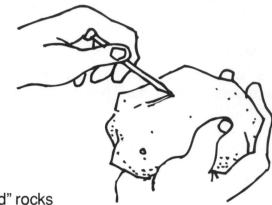

Materials

- assorted rocks (including soft stones such as pumice, talc, sandstone)
- coin
- large nail

Steps to Follow

1. Students feel the rocks and sort them into piles—"hard" rocks in one pile and "soft" rocks in another.
2. Select students to scratch rocks in this order:
    a. Scratch with a fingernail. Place any rocks they can mark in a pile and set aside.
    b. Scratch remaining rocks with a coin. Place any rocks with coin marks in a separate pile.
    c. Scratch remaining rocks with a large nail. Place any rocks with nail marks in a third pile.
    d. Place any unmarked rocks in a fourth pile.
3. Ask:
    a. Are all rocks hard?
    b. Do softer rocks look different than harder rocks?
    c. How did you decide which rocks were the hardest?
4. Add discoveries to the class logbook page entitled "Rock Properties." Have each student use a copy of page 5 to record results in individual logs.

Buoyancy

This investigation shows that not all rocks sink.

Materials

- rocks (include lava, pumice)
- clear container
- water
- paper towels

Steps to Follow

1. Have students predict which rocks will float and which will sink.
2. Put the rocks in a container of water one at a time to verify their predictions.
3. Ask:
    a. Did all the rocks sink?
    b. What did the rocks that floated look like?
    c. Can you think of other heavy things that float?
4. Add discoveries to the class logbook page entitled "Rock Properties." Have each student use a copy of page 5 to record results for individual logs.

Rock Properties

Teach students the term "properties"— distinctive characteristics or qualities belonging to something. Give some examples, such as:

Properties of a pine tree are cones and needles.
Properties of a bird are feathers and two legs.
Properties of water are that it flows and takes the shape of whatever it is poured into.

Review the properties of rocks that have been previously explored:
color and pattern
hardness
buoyancy

Divide the students into small groups. Explain that each group is going to list the properties of a rock in a way that everyone in the class can understand. For example, if a group says the rock is "hard," they must define it in such a way that classmates can check the property. *(Hard means it can't be scratched by a nail. Hard means I can't break it with a hammer. Hard means it makes a scratch on other rocks.)*

1. Give each group a rock and each student a copy of page 35.
2. Have students work together to think of three properties that their rock possesses.
3. Have them record the properties and definitions on the group's copy of page 35.
4. Provide time for a student from each group to show the group's rock and share its properties.
5. Make additions and corrections to the class logbook.

Extension Activity

Invite a rock hound or geologist to speak to the class about rocks and their properties. Prepare the class by practicing the skill of asking questions and listening carefully to the answers.

Write thank-you notes to the speaker. Have students include at least one fact they learned from the speaker in their notes.

Types of Rocks for Your Classroom Collection

• igneous — granite, quartz, basalt, obsidian, feldspar, lava, pumice
• metamorphic — slate, gneiss, marble, quartzite
• sedimentary — sandstone, shale, limestone, gypsum, flint

If you need to purchase rocks to extend your collection, try lapidary shops, building suppliers, nature stores, and educational supply catalogs.

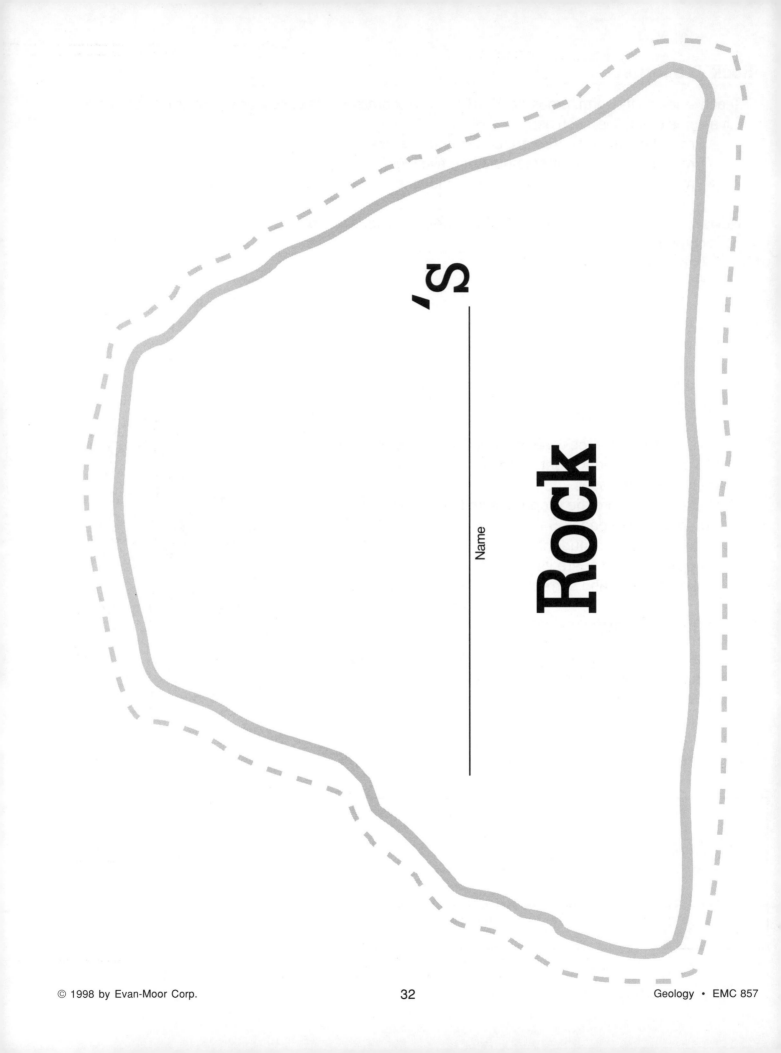

_____
Name

Rock

's

This is my rock.

I found it _____

_____

1

Describe your rock.

How does it look and feel?

_____

2

Note: Reproduce this page for students to use with the activity on page 31.

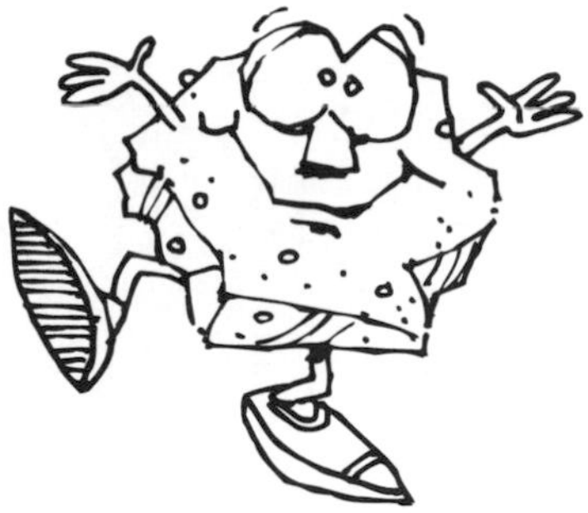

Name ______________________________

The Properties of a Rock

Draw the rock.

List three properties of the rock.
Tell what each property means.

1. ______________________________

____

2. ______________________________

____

3. ______________________________

____

Rocks are formed in different ways.

Thinking About Rocks

Place books about rocks with your classroom rock collection. Add a sign that asks, "How are rocks made?" Give students a chance to examine the materials for several days before beginning the activities in this section.

Cooking Up Rocks

- Sit the class together. Pass around several rocks of different types. Ask, "How are they different? How do you think rocks are made?" Record student descriptions of rock formation on a page in the class logbook.

- Explain that although we can't make rocks, we can use cooking to get an idea of how different types of rocks are formed.

  With students acting as assistants, demonstrate any or all of the cooking experiences on pages 37–39. The recipes include Lollipop Rocks, Munchies, and Lot-O-Layers.

Lollipop Rocks

When melted rock (magma) pushes through the Earth's crust it cools into a solid (igneous) rock. In this cooking demonstration, students will see how this occurs.

To avoid any possibility of burns from hot liquid, make a circle of masking tape a safe distance around the demonstration table. Students stay outside the circle unless invited by the teacher to act as an assistant. No one should be in the circle when you are working with the hot liquid.

Explain to students that this demonstration will show how one kind of rock is formed. They are to observe what happens when the hot liquid cools.

Ingredients

- 3 cups (600 g) sugar
- 3/4 cup (177 ml) light corn syrup
- 3 tablespoons (45 ml) white vinegar
- 1/3 cup (79 ml) boiling water
- few drops red food coloring

Materials

- a large saucepan
- wooden skewers (cut off sharp tips)
- a candy thermometer
- a wooden spoon
- a cookie sheet (greased)
- a heat source

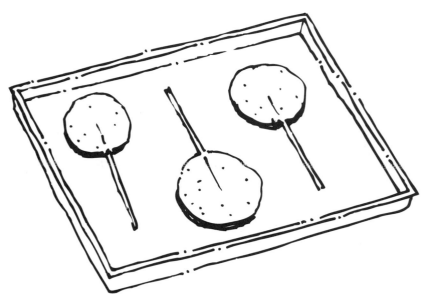

Steps to Follow

1. Combine sugar, corn syrup, vinegar, and water. Stir until sugar dissolves.
2. Cook to the hard-crack stage (300° F or 150° C).
3. Remove from heat. Add food coloring.
4. Cool until slightly thick.
5. Place skewers 5" (13 cm) apart on the greased cookie sheet.
6. Drop candy from a spoon over one end of skewers to form 3" (7.5 cm) lollipops.

Follow Up

At the conclusion of the demonstration, ask students to describe what they observed. *(The boiling hot liquid became hard when it cooled.)* Explain that rocks formed when melted rock cools and becomes solid are called **igneous rocks**.

> **Important:**
> Show students an example of an igneous rock (obsidian, quartz, granite). Ask them to explain how the rock and the lollipops are alike.

 Geology • EMC 857

Munchies

A metamorphic rock is created when heat and pressure change a soft rock like limestone into a much harder rock like marble. Here is a "munchie" that changes from a soft form to a harder form through heat.

Explain to students that this demonstration will show how one kind of rock is formed. Have students feel samples of the soft cookies before they are baked a second time. Feel the "munchies" again after they cool. (You may want to do the first stage of baking [up through step 6] in advance to speed up the process.)

Materials

- wooden spoon
- hand mixer
- small mixing bowl
- large mixing bowl
- 2 cookie sheets
- parchment paper
- heat source

Ingredients

- 4 cups (500 g) flour (sifted)
- 2 teaspoons (8 g) baking powder
- 1/2 teaspoon (2 g) baking soda
- 1/2 teaspoon (2 g) salt
- 2 cups (400 g) sugar
- 4 large eggs
- 3/4 cup (177 ml) oil
- 1 teaspoon (5 ml) vanilla

Steps to Follow

1. Mix flour, baking powder, baking soda, and salt together in the small mixing bowl.
2. Beat the eggs in the large mixing bowl. Add sugar, oil, and vanilla to the eggs.
3. Add the flour mixture a little at a time to the egg mixture. (It will become very stiff. An adult will need to take over the final mixing if using student assistants.)
4. Dump the mixture out onto a floured surface. Form the dough into six balls.
5. Line the cookie sheets with parchment paper. Roll each ball into a "snake" as long as the cookie sheet. Lay three "snakes" on each sheet. Flatten the snakes with your fingers.
6. Bake at 375° F(175° C) for 25 minutes or until golden brown. Remove from oven. Let cool until you can pry the strips of parchment off the back.
7. Cut the cookies diagonally. Turn them on their sides and return to the parchment paper.
8. Bake for an additional 10 minutes.
9. Let cookies cool.

Follow Up

At the conclusion of the demonstration, ask students to describe how the cookies changed after being baked again. *(The soft cookies became much harder.)* Explain that soft rocks such as sedimentary rocks that are squeezed and heated for a long time change into harder metamorphic rocks.

Important:
As students are enjoying their metamorphic munchies, show an example of softer rock and the **metamorphic rock** it becomes (shale to slate, limestone to marble, granite to gneiss). Ask students to explain how the rock and the munchies are alike.

Lot-O-Layers

Sedimentary rocks are made in layers. The layers of mud, sand, or even seashells are built up over a long time. The layers get squeezed and stuck together to make new rocks. This cookie retains the layers even when cooked.

Explain to students that this demonstration will show how one kind of rock is formed. They are to observe how the layers are laid in the pan. Then observe the finished product to see what, if any, changes have occurred.

Ingredients

- 1/2 cup (113 g) butter
- 1 1/2 cups (185 g) vanilla wafer crumbs
- 1 14 oz. (414 ml) can sweetened condensed milk
- 1 6 oz. (170 g) package chocolate chips
- 1 6 oz. (170 g) package peanut butter chips
- 1 cup (113 g) chopped nuts

Materials

- clear 13" x 9" (33 x 23 cm) baking pan
- can opener
- heat source

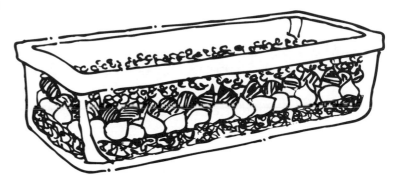

Steps to Follow

1. Melt the butter in the baking pan.
2. Sprinkle crumbs over the butter.
3. Pour condensed milk evenly over the crumbs.
4. Layer the remaining ingredients evenly over the top.
5. Press down gently. Bake at 350° F (175° C) 25 – 30 minutes or until lightly brown.
6. Let cool. Cut into bars.

Follow Up

At the conclusion of the demonstration, ask students to describe how the cooked item was formed. (Layers of ingredients were put in the pan. The ingredients melted some, but they were still in layers.) Explain that rocks formed when layers are squeezed together over a long period of time are called **sedimentary rocks**.

Important:
Show an example of a sedimentary rock (sandstone, shale, limestone, gypsum, flint). Ask students to explain how the rock and the cookie are alike.

Summary Activities

- Reproduce the minibook on pages 42–44. Read the pages together to review the types of rocks — igneous, sedimentary, metamorphic — and how they are made. (Don't expect students to remember all of this information.)

- Record student explanations in the class logbook. Have students copy the information for their individual logs, using the form on page 4.

- Read appropriate sections from books such as *Rocks and Minerals — A New True Book* by Illa Podendorf (Children's Press, 1982) and *Rock Collecting* by Roma Gans (Harper and Row, 1984) for an additional confirmation of how each type of rock is made.

Extension Activities

- Invite a rock expert to help students identify some of the rocks they collected. Label the rocks for a class collection.

- Visit a natural history museum with a rock collection.

- Pass around a conglomerate rock. Ask students to describe what they see. *(It looks like bits of stuff glued together.)* Make conglomerate rocks by gluing bits and pieces together following the directions on page 41. Or, if you have not exhausted your cooking urges, whip up a batch of "Chewy Conglomerates" — also on page 41.

How Rocks Are Made

Some rocks are cooled magma.

Some rocks are made in layers.

Some rocks change from soft to hard.

It takes a long time.

THESE LOOK LIKE BITS OF STUFF GLUED TOGETHER.

Conglomerate ROCKS

Make Conglomerate Rocks

Follow these steps to make a conglomerate.

Materials

- tiny rocks and bits of shell
- white glue
- waxed paper
- ice cream stick

Steps to Follow

1. Place a small amount of rocks and shells in a pile on the waxed paper.
2. Add a small amount of white glue and stir until well mixed.
3. Let dry completely.

Chewy Conglomerates

A conglomerate is a rock composed of bits and pieces of other kinds of rocks cemented together with mud and sand. This conglomerate is guaranteed to taste better.

Ingredients

- one-half pound of milk chocolate bars
- 1 1/2 cups (76 g) miniature marshmallows
- 1/2 cup (57 g) coarsely chopped walnuts
- 1/2 cup (15 g) crisp rice cereal

Materials

- double boiler
- cookie sheet
- wooden spoon
- heat source

Steps to Follow

1. Place the chocolate bars in a pan and soften them over a pan of hot water.
2. Remove from heat and stir the chocolate until it is smooth.
3. Fold in the marshmallows, nuts, and cereal.
4. Drop by the spoonful onto a buttered cookie sheet.
5. Chill before serving.

Geology • EMC 857

Name _____

How Rocks Are Made

All rocks are a part of the Earth's crust.

When the Earth was first formed, melted rock called **magma** pushed up through cracks in the Earth's crust. The melted rock cooled and hardened.

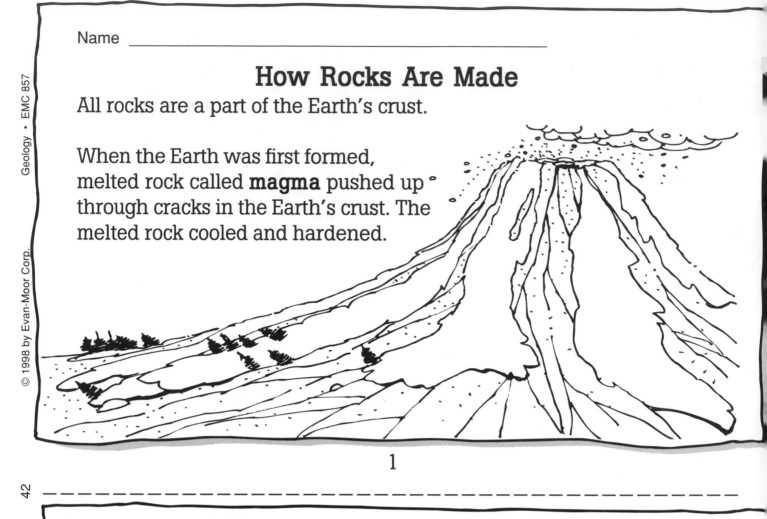

1

Igneous rocks still come from magma under the ground. Some igneous rock cools slowly underground. Some cool quickly on the surface.

Granite comes from magma. Granite is speckled. Some of the speckles shine. It is a heavy rock.

Basalt comes from magma. It is a black, heavy rock.

Pumice comes from lava shot out of a volcano. It cools with air bubbles in it. Because of the bubbles, it floats.

2

Sedimentary rocks are made from bits of rock that have been pressed together. These rocks are made underwater. Layers of mud, sand, or even sea shells are built up over a long time. The layers get squeezed and stuck together to make new rocks. Many sedimentary rocks contain fossils.

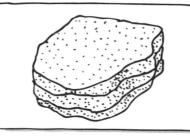

Sandstone is made of layers of sand that have been squeezed into rock.

Shale is mud that has been squeezed into rock.

Limestone is made of sea shells. The sea shells sank to the bottom of the sea where they were pressed and stuck together.

3

Rocks can be made in one more way. Sedimentary rocks can be changed by time, heat, and pressure under the surface of the Earth. These become **metamorphic** rocks.

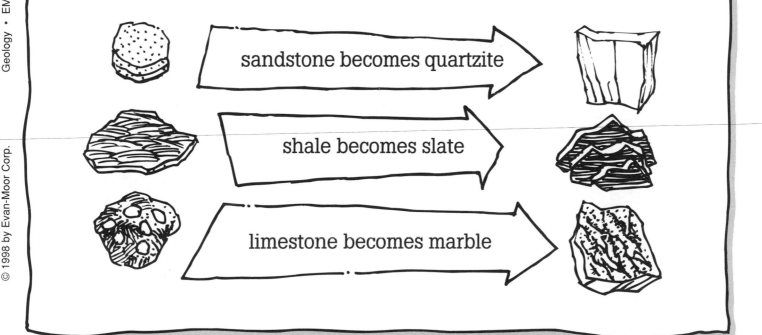

sandstone becomes quartzite

shale becomes slate

limestone becomes marble

4

How much time does it take? — If you squeeze and heat a rock for a few million years, it can turn into a new kind of rock.

Where does the heat come from? — When rocks are close enough to the magma to be heated but not close enough to be melted, the rocks can be changed.

Where does the pressure come from? — Rocks below the surface are squeezed by the layers of rock above them. The thicker the layers, the more pressure there is.

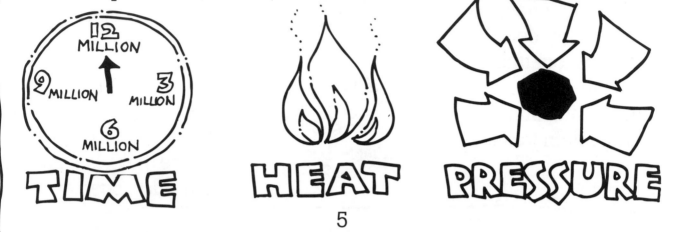

5

People use rocks for many things. Coal, used for energy, comes from certain rocks. Some buildings are made of rock. Rocks contain metals such as gold and silver. Some rocks contain stones that are polished and used in jewelry.

Granite is a hard rock used to build roads. Clay is a soft rock used to make pottery and bricks. Talc is a very soft rock used to make chalk and talcum powder.

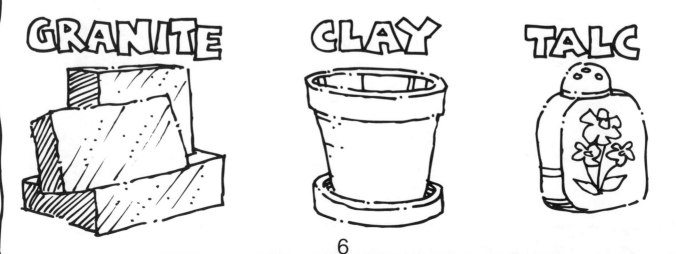

6

The surface of the Earth is always changing.

Sandbox Landscape—An Introductory Activity

Reproduce the letter on page 48 for each student to take home the day before the lesson. The letter asks parents to send their children to school in play clothes as they will be working with damp sand during science class.

1. Supply students with buckets and small trowels and take them to the outdoor sandbox. (To make sand easier to work with, get permission to dampen it beforehand.)
2. Challenge students to build a landscape of mountains, rivers, and smooth flat places.
3. When they have finished, have everyone sit around the outside of the sandbox. Ask, "What did you do to change the surface of the sand? How did you make the changes?"
   I dug a river down the middle.
   I pushed up a pile of sand to make a mountain.
   I smoothed that spot flat.
4. To explore land forms around you, conduct one of the following activities:
   • Walk around the neighborhood to observe surface features (flat areas, depressions, hills in the distance, river bed, etc.). Ask, "How do you think the (mountain, river, flat space, etc.) was made?"
   • Prepare a video of surface features in your area. Show the video and ask, "How do you think these features were made?"

Erosion

Moving Soil Center

Preparation

Set up an exploration center. Post the directions chart on page 49. Have a whisk broom, dustpan, and plenty of paper towels available for cleanup.

Materials

- plastic watering can or cup with a lip
- baking sheet (with a rim)
- washtub
- newspaper to cover work area
- scoop
- pitcher or bottle of water
- block of wood
- bucket (for dumping used soil)
- supply of soil (must be fine, dry soil)
- paper towels (for cleanup)
- directions chart on page 49
- logbook form on page 5, reproduced for each student

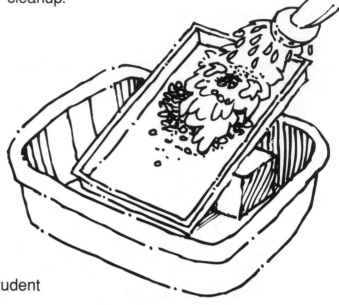

Steps to Follow

1. Explain the steps on the chart.
2. Demonstrate how to use the materials.
3. Provide time for small groups to explore the effects of water and wind on soil.
4. Students record the investigations on copies of page 5.

Follow Up

- Discuss what students observed during their explorations.
  "What happened when you blew across the soil?"
  (Some of the soil blew away.)
  "What causes soil to blow away outside?"
  (The wind.)
  "What happened when you poured water on the soil?"
  (Some of the soil washed away.)
  "How does water wash away soil outside?"
  (Rain falls and washes soil away. Rivers wash soil away.)
- Record their discoveries in the class logbook on a page entitled "Wind and Water."

Wind and Water

Wind blows away sand and dirt.

Water washes away sand and dirt.

The land looks different.

Saving the Soil

- Ask students to think of ways they might keep soil from being blown or washed away. Record their suggestions on the chalkboard. (You will probably get suggestions such as build a wall, use rocks, plant things, dig a hole to catch the water, etc.)

- Repeat the water and wind experiment described on page 46 to demonstrate as many of your students' suggestions as possible. Some will keep the soil from moving but will create other problems. (Example: A wall will keep the soil beyond the wall from washing away, but water will back up causing a flood.) Others will successfully slow down the erosion of the soil. (Both pebbles and plants will help cut down on the amount of soil washed away.)

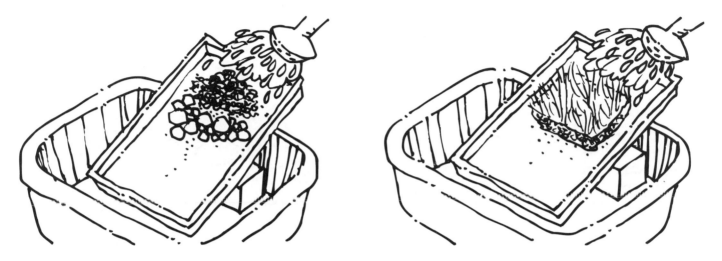

- Record the results in the class logbook and in individual logs, using the form on page 5.

- Discuss the effect of erosion on crops. Visit a farm (or invite a farmer to speak to the class) to learn how farmers minimize erosion of their fields.

- Make overhead transparencies of pages 50 and 51. Show one transparency at a time. Ask students to describe the changes they see and to explain how the changes occurred.

- Reproduce page 52 for each student to complete. This serves as an additional way to assess student understanding of the concept.

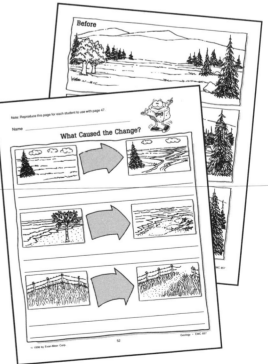

- Reproduce the minibook on pages 53 and 54 for each student. Read and discuss the book together. Make any other needed changes in the class and individual logs.

Geology • EMC 857

Dear Parents,

As part of our study of geology, we are exploring how wind and water change the surface of the Earth. Tomorrow we will be working with wet sand during our investigation. Please have your child wear play clothes for the day.

Sincerely,

Dear Parents,

As part of our study of geology, we are exploring how wind and water change the surface of the Earth. Tomorrow we will be working with wet sand during our investigation. Please have your child wear play clothes for the day.

Sincerely,

How Do Wind and Water Change the Earth?

1 fill the tray with soil

2 blow

3 put tray and block in tub

4 pour water

5 dump soil in can

6 write in log

 Geology • EMC 857

Before

After

Geology • EMC 857

Before

After

51

Geology • EMC 857

Name _____

What Caused the Change?

_____

_____

_____

_____

Geology • EMC 857

How Does the Earth's Surface Change?

Moving water changes the land.
It moves soil, sand, and rocks to new places.

1

Moving wind changes the land.
It blows soil and sand to new places.

2

Moving ice can change the land.
It cuts out places as it moves.
It breaks apart rocks.

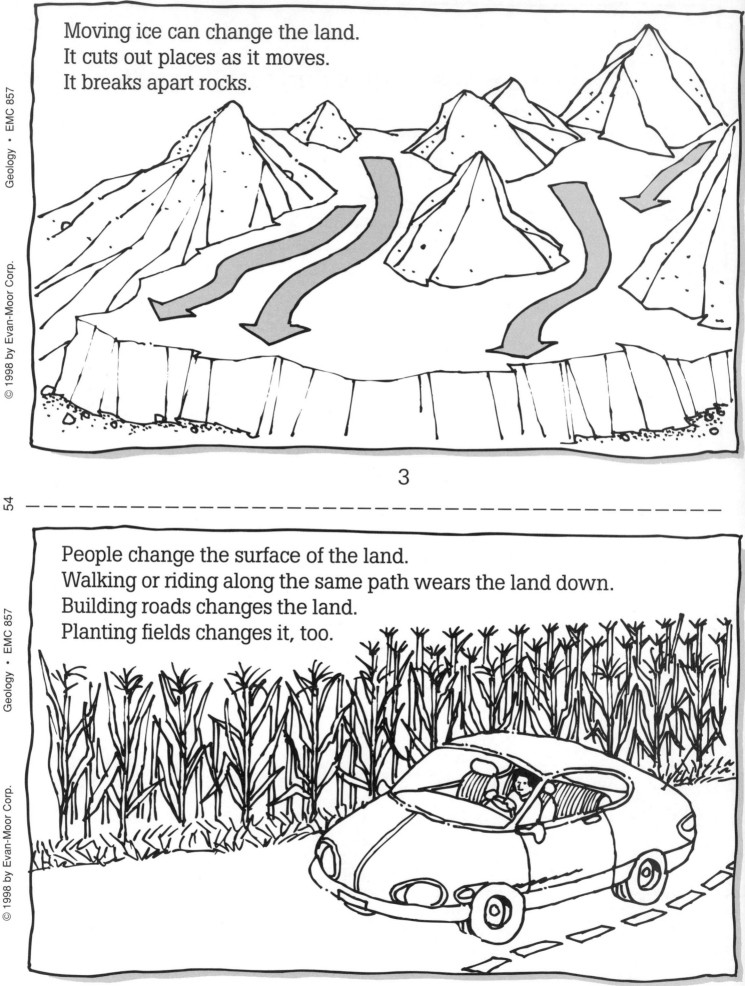

3

People change the surface of the land.
Walking or riding along the same path wears the land down.
Building roads changes the land.
Planting fields changes it, too.

4

Volcanoes

Have students assist as you demonstrate the following volcano "eruption."

Materials

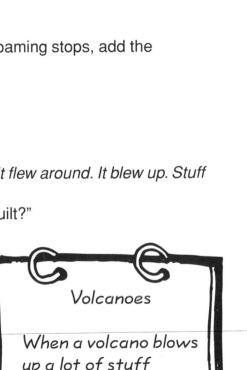

- modeling clay
- small plastic cup
- 1 tablespoon (8 g) flour
- 2 tablespoons (16 g) baking soda
- 1/3 cup (80 ml) vinegar
- 4" (10 cm) square of tissue paper
- optional: add a drop of red food coloring to the vinegar
- paper towels (for cleanup)
- apron
- safety goggles
- large cookie sheet

Steps to Follow

Select different students to help with each step. The student assisting with step four needs to wear an apron and safety goggles.

1. Build a volcano shape with the clay on the cookie sheet. Make an opening in the top large enough to hold the small plastic cup.
2. Put the baking soda and flour in the center of the tissue paper. Wrap the paper around the mixture, and twist both ends tightly.
3. Place the mixture in the cup.
4. Pour half of the vinegar into the hole and step back. When the foaming stops, add the remaining vinegar.

Follow Up

- After the volcano erupts, ask questions such as:

    "What did you see when the volcano erupted?"

    "What happened to the foam that came out of the volcano?" *(It flew around. It blew up. Stuff landed on the sides of the volcano.)*

    "What does this show us about how a volcanic mountain is built?"

- Record student comments in the class logbook on a page entitled "Volcanoes."

- Read *Facts about Volcanoes* by Jane Walker (Millbrook Press, 1995) or show a video such as *Born of Fire* from the National Geographic Society. Ask students to share their new information about volcanoes. Correct any misinformation. Make corrections and additions to the class logbook page. Use the form on page 4 for students to write about volcanoes for their individual logs.

- Reproduce page 57 for each student. They are to label the parts of a volcano.

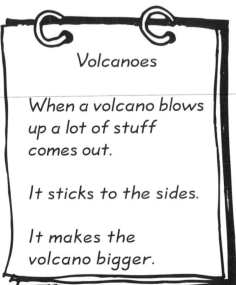

Volcanoes

When a volcano blows up a lot of stuff comes out.

It sticks to the sides.

It makes the volcano bigger.

Earthquakes

- Explain that earthquakes are also a way the Earth is built up. Read *How Mountains Are Made* by Kathleen Weidner Zoehfeld (Harper Collins, 1995) or *Earthquakes* by Franklyn M. Branley (Thomas Y. Crowell, 1990). Ask students to share what they learned about mountain formation from listening to the story.

- Reproduce the map on page 58 for each student to use as they explore the ways the Earth can move during an earthquake.

  1. Have students push their paper maps together from the sides. Ask:
     "What happened to your map?" *(It pushed up.)*
     "What have you made?" *(a hill)*
     "Sometimes an earthquake makes the land fold like this."
  2. Have students cut the fault line of their maps with scissors. Then push the two sides of the papers toward each other. Ask:
     "What happened to your map?" *(One side came up. It crumpled over on top of the other piece.)*
     "Sometimes an earthquake pushes one piece of land over another piece."

  3. Have students slide one side of the map forward and the other side backward. Ask:
     "What happened to your map?" *(The pieces go in different directions.)*
     "Sometimes an earthquake causes pieces of land to move away from each other."

Then describe what students learned about earthquakes in the class logbook and have them record their observations in individual logs, using copies of the form on page 4.

- Reproduce the minibook on pages 59 and 60 to further confirm student understanding of earthquakes and volcanoes.

- Earthquake Safety
  Scientists can give a warning about a volcanic eruption so people can leave a dangerous area. There are no clear signs that an earthquake is about to happen. People living in earthquake territory need to understand how to be safe when one occurs. Read *Be Ready, Be Safe for Earthquakes* by Libby Lafferty and Tina Lafferty (Lafferty and Associates, 1994) to share safety tips with students. Practice these if you live in an earthquake area.

Geology • EMC 857

Name _____

The Parts of a Volcano

Color the hot lava coming out of the volcano.

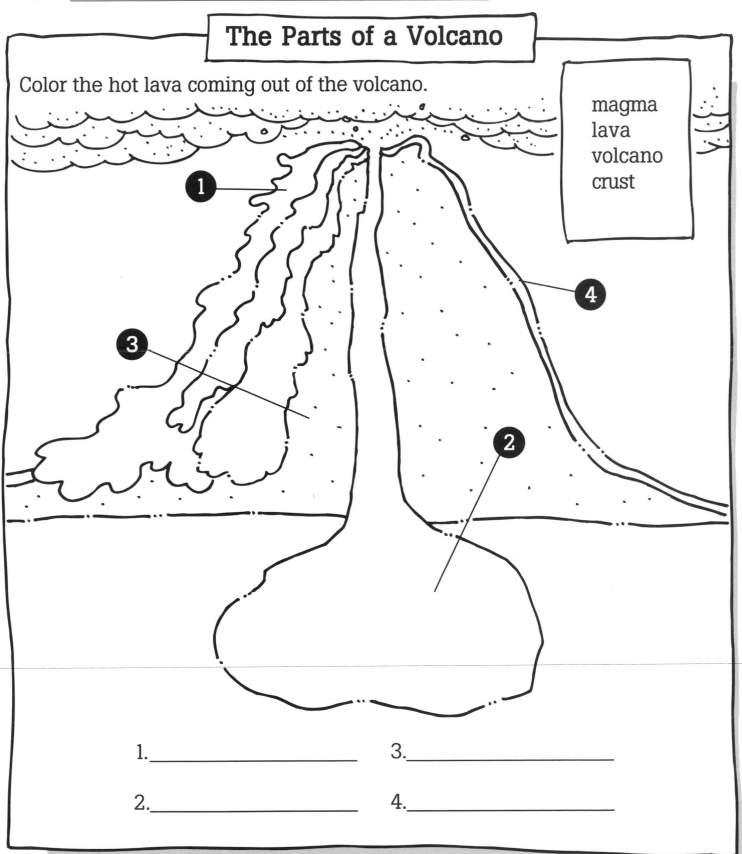

magma
lava
volcano
crust

1. _____   3. _____

2. _____   4. _____

Make Your Own Earthquakes

Name _____

Earthquakes and Volcanoes

The Earth's crust is broken into pieces like a big puzzle. These pieces are called **plates**. The plates move slowly. This moving changes the surface of the Earth. This movement also causes earthquakes and volcanoes.

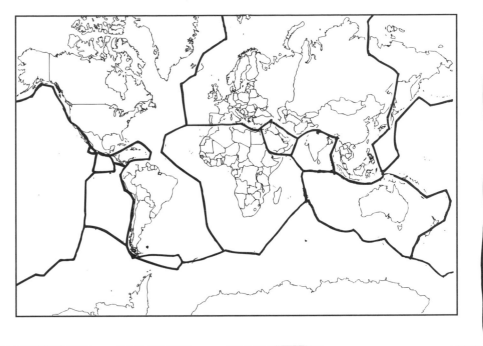

1

Plates can move away from each other. When this happens, **magma** flows up through the cracks, making a volcano.

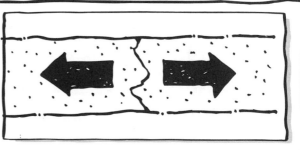

Plates can move toward each other. The movement can cause an earthquake as the crust is pushed up. Or cracks are made in the crust letting magma flow through, making a volcano. These are the two ways mountains are made.

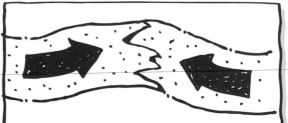

Plates can slip past each other. This movement of the crust also causes earthquakes.

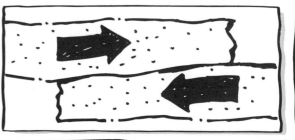

2

This mountain was made by a volcano.

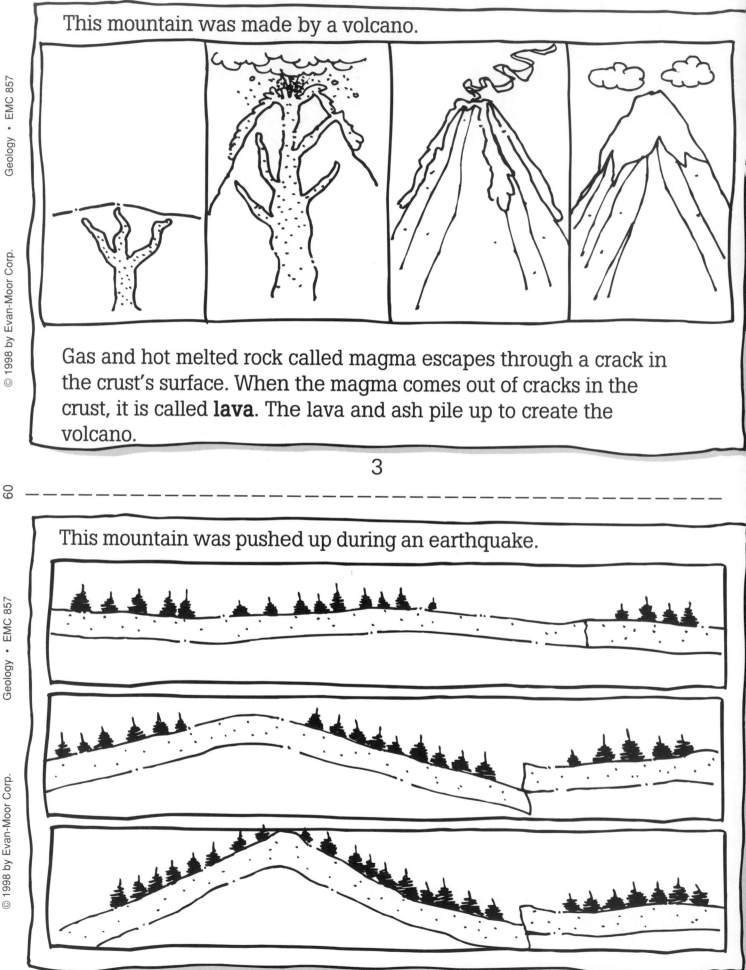

Gas and hot melted rock called magma escapes through a crack in the crust's surface. When the magma comes out of cracks in the crust, it is called **lava**. The lava and ash pile up to create the volcano.

3

This mountain was pushed up during an earthquake.

4

The resources we use come from the Earth.

Where Does It Come From?

Engage students in a discussion of yesterday's home and school activities. Ask, "What did you use when you (ate breakfast, etc.)?" List these on a chart.

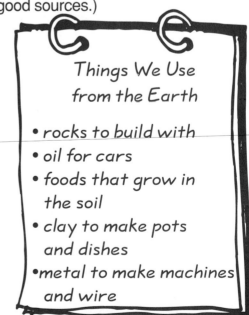

I ate breakfast. *(cereal in a bowl, milk, banana, spoon)*
I came to school. *(walked in sneakers, rode my bicycle)*
I went with my dad to the gas station. *(car, pump, gasoline)*
I watched TV. *(television set, electricity, TV Guide)*
I painted a picture. *(paint, brush, paper)*
I wrote on the chalkboard. *(chalkboard, chalk, eraser)*

Read each item on the list and ask students to decide if it came from the Earth. Circle an item if they respond "Yes." Do not correct wrong responses at this time. Save the list.

Using Earth's Resources

• View filmstrips or videos relating to the Earth's resources (formation and use of coal, mining and smelting of ores, formation of goods from petroleum by-products, etc.), or read selections from books about natural resources. (*Eyewitness Books; Rocks & Minerals* by Dr. R. F. Symes and staff of the Natural History Museum, London [Alfred A. Knopf, 1998] and *Material Resources* by Robin Kerrod [Thomson Learning, 1994] are two good sources.)

• After sharing information, ask students to recall what they learned about how we use things (resources) that come from the Earth.

Record their comments in the class logbook on a page entitled "Things We Use from the Earth." Have students write about what they are learning in their individual logs, using copies of the form on page 4.

Return to the list on the chart started earlier. Read through the items again. Ask students what changes need to be made. Correct any misconceptions.

Things We Use from the Earth

• rocks to build with
• oil for cars
• foods that grow in the soil
• clay to make pots and dishes
• metal to make machines and wire

Follow Up

• Reproduce the minibook on pages 66–69 for each student. Read and complete the pages together to verify knowledge and to correct misinformation.

• Work with students to write a definition of "resource" as it relates to the Earth. Record it in the class logbook on a chart entitled "A resource is..."

• Reproduce page 64 for each student. They are to match the resource with something we use that is made from it.

• Take a walking trip around the neighborhood to find examples of things that come from a natural resource. Reproduce page 65 for each student to use to record the examples they find.

Use pieces of sturdy cardboard to make "clipboards" for students to take on the walk. Staple the form to the cardboard and attach a pencil with string.

A resource is anything from the Earth like rocks, oil, and clay that we use or make into other things to use.

Geology • EMC 857

Sharing Earth's Resources

- Read *Common Ground — The Water, Earth, and Air We Share* by Molly Bang (Blue Sky Press, 1997) to introduce the idea that we need to use our Earth's resources wisely.

- Write a page for the class logbook entitled "We Share the Earth."

- Discuss ways we can use the Earth's resources more carefully. List students' ideas on a chart for the class logbook. Have students write about conserving resources in their individual logs.

We Share the Earth

We share the land, air, and water.

We share with other people.

We share with animals.

We share with plants.

Make Conservation Posters

Have students paint posters using some of their ideas for conserving resources. Post these around school to remind everyone to use our natural resources wisely.

Materials

- 18" x 24" (45.5 x 61 cm) posterboard or heavy construction paper
- paint and brushes (for illustrations)
- wide marking pens (for lettering)

Steps to Follow

1. Prepare a painting area, including a place for posters to dry.
2. Discuss what could go on the posters.
3. Have students select a topic and plan their poster on scratch paper. (Some students may want to work with a partner.)
4. Provide time for everyone to complete a poster.
5. Once the posters are dry, post them around the school (with Principal's permission) or around the neighborhood (with permission from the owner of the place the poster will be displayed).

Geology • EMC 857

Name _____

Where Does It Come From?

Match.

minerals

soil

clay

petroleum

limestone and sand

GAS

Name _____

How Is It Used?

Draw or write something you saw made from these:

rock

metal

clay

Other resources I saw being used:

_____   _____

_____   _____

The Earth Gives Us What We Need

People have learned how to use the natural resources that are found in the Earth's crust. Let's learn about some of the resources we use.

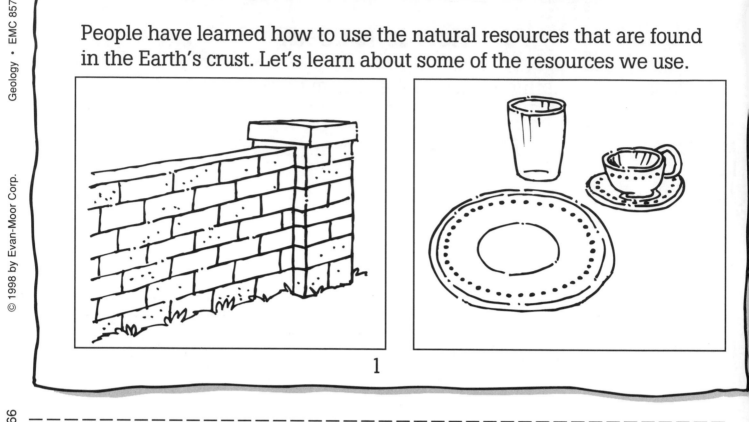

1

Rocks

We use rocks for many things. Fences, chimneys, and walls are built of cut stones. Statues and monuments are made of polished stones like marble. A hard rock called granite is use to build roads. Precious stones like diamonds are made into jewelry.

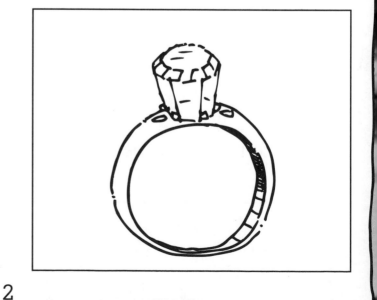

2

Some Rocks are Changed

Clay is soft and can be easily shaped into pots, dishes, or other forms. When the clay is baked in a special oven, it becomes very hard.

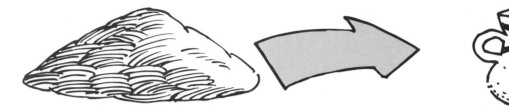

Did you know that glass is made from rocks? Sand and limestone are melted together. While the glass is still hot and soft, it can be stretched into panes of glass or shaped into glass objects.

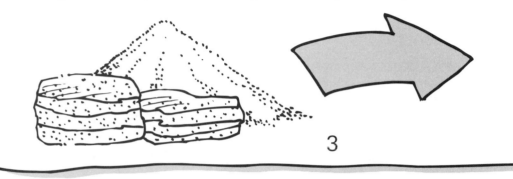

3

Coal

One of the most useful rocks is coal. People in many parts of the world burn coal for fuel. Coal was made from trees and plants that died millions of years ago. They were covered in mud and sand. As time passed, they were slowly turned into rocks called coal.

4

Petroleum

Petroleum is a dark, oily liquid found in the Earth. It was made from living things that died and were buried in mud and sand. After millions of years they turned into drops of oil.

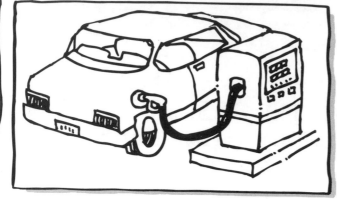

Many products we use are petroleum. Gasoline and oil for cars and other machines come from petroleum.

Petroleum is even used to make plastic. The plastic is turned into all kinds of things we use every day.

5

Soil

Soil is one of the Earth's most important resources. Much of the food we eat comes from plants that grow in the soil. Trees cut to make lumber for our homes grow in soil.

6

Metals

Many metals are found in rocks. Sometimes a metal is used by itself. Sometimes several metals are mixed together before being used.

Steel is made from the metal iron. The steel is used in buildings and in all kind of machines.

Aluminum is light and strong. It is used in building large machines like airplanes. It is used to make small things like soda cans.

Copper is used to make wire used in electrical equipment. It is easy to stretch without breaking, and it doesn't rust.

7

Do You Remember?

Name one thing that is made from each natural resource.

1. clay _____

2. rock _____

3. metal _____

4. petroleum _____

5. sand and limestone _____

8

Some rocks contain fossils that tell about life on Earth long ago.

Secrets in Rocks

- Display a magnifying glass and a rock containing a fossil. Add a sign saying, "What Is in This Rock?" Let students discover the fossil on their own.

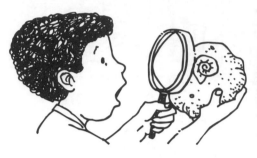

  After several days, call the class together and hold up the rock. Ask, "What did you find in this rock?" Continue your questioning until someone answers "a fossil."

- Put out a set of rocks with and without fossils. (If you don't have access to rocks with fossils, reproduce the cards on pages 78–80 to use with this lesson.) Have students examine the rocks and divide them into two sets — rocks with fossils and rocks without fossils. Have students tell how they knew which rocks contained fossils. Then ask them to explain how they think the fossils got there.

Fossils

Fossils are dead animals that lived a long time ago.

Fossils can be plants.

They can be dinosaur footprints, too.

- Have students write a definition of "fossil" to go in the class logbook.

- Reproduce these pages for students to complete:
    - Page 73 — Students find and color the fossils found in a large rock.
    - Page 74 —Students match the fossil to the plant or animal that made it.

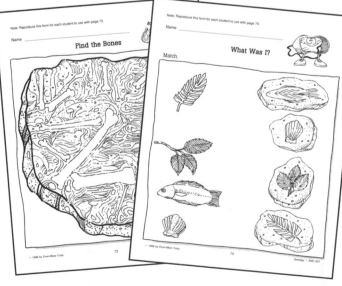

How Fossils Are Made

- Read *Fossils Tell of Long Ago* by Aliki (Harper and Row, 1990). Have students add new information and make corrections to the class logbook and in their individual logs.

- Reproduce the fossil minibook on pages 75 and 76 for each student. Have them read and complete the pages.

- Reproduce page 77 for each student. Have them study the fossils at the top of the page and then complete the page.

Extension Activities

- Invite a guest speaker (scientist, paleontologist, natural museum curator, etc.) to talk to the class about fossils. If possible, visit a natural history museum to see a collection of fossils.

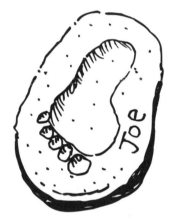

- While following the directions on page 72, explain to students that they are making "fossil" footprints of their own feet. Remind them that it took millions of years for dinosaur footprints to become fossils. They will be making a model of a fossil. After completing the steps on page 72, have students explain how their footprints are like and unlike real fossils.

         Geology • EMC 857

Fossil Footprints

Materials

- self-hardening clay
  (available at craft shops)
- paper towels
- newspaper
- pencil

Steps to Follow

1. Give each student a lump of clay about the size of an orange, a newspaper, and two paper towels.

2. Place the clay on the newspaper and press it out flat to a size slightly larger than their right foot. Place the newspaper and clay on the floor.

3. Take off the right shoe and sock. Step on the clay firmly and then carefully lift the foot away, leaving a print.

4. Students write their names in the clay.

5. Set the footprints aside to dry for several days.

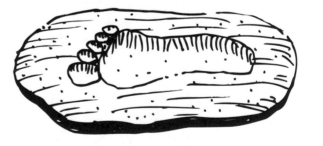

Geology • EMC 857

Note: Reproduce this form for each student to use with page 70.

Name _____

Find the Bones

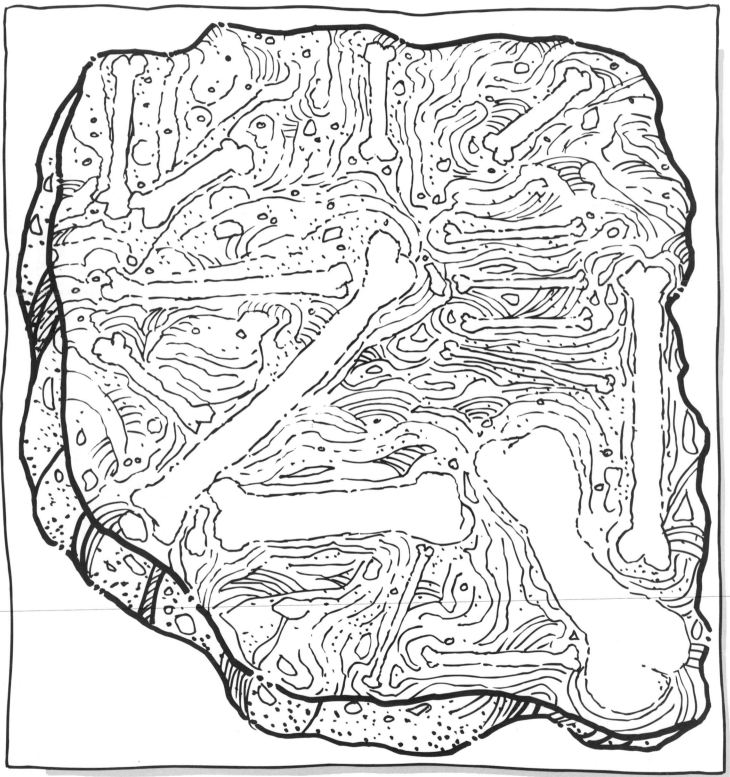

Geology • EMC 857

Name _____

What Was I?

Match.

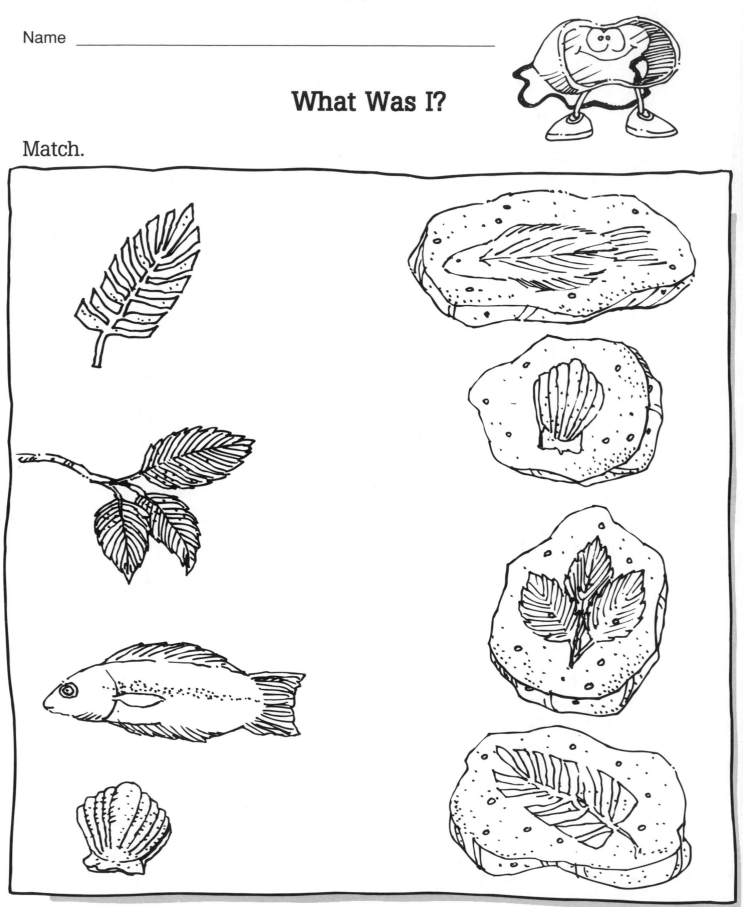

Fossils Tell about the Earth of Long Ago

Fossils are the hardened remains of animals or plants that lived on the Earth long before there were any people. Scientists study these fossils to find out about ancient life.

Fossils of animals and plants from both land and sea have been found.

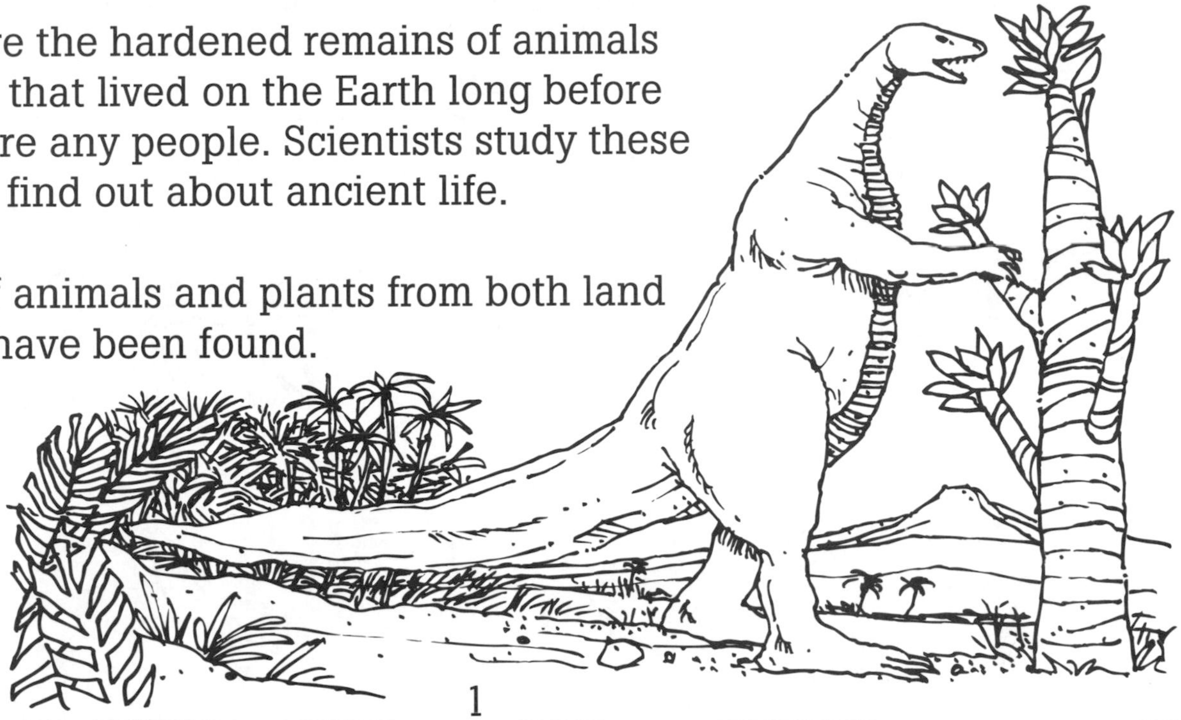

1

After the animal or plant died, all of the soft parts decayed and disappeared. The hard parts remained lying on the ground. Some of the hard parts were covered with sand, mud, or water.

2

Over a long, long time, minerals seeped in and took the place of the bone or other part. What was left was a rock in the same shape.

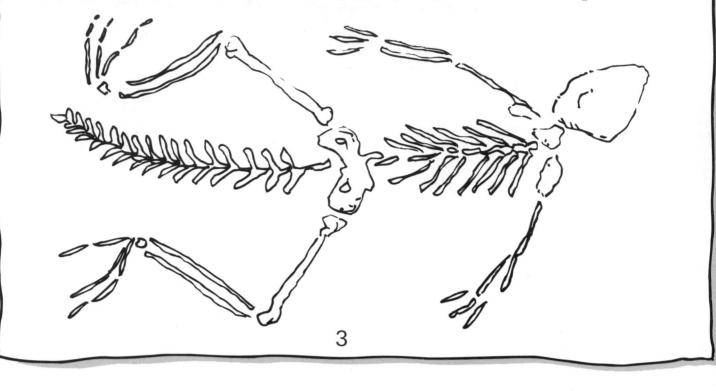

3

The largest fossils found are prints left after a dinosaur died. There are fossils of whole skeletons and nests of dinosaur eggs. Bones, teeth, footprints, and prints of skin have all been found.

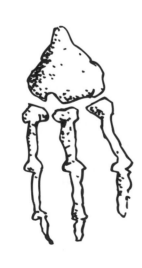
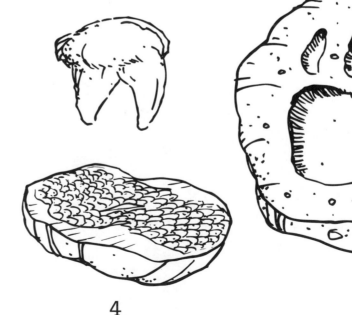

4

Name _____

Fossils

Write the name of the kind of animal that left the fossil.

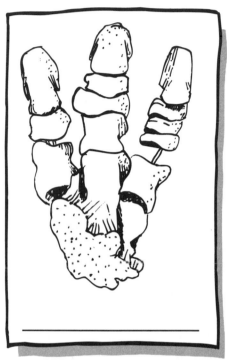

_____

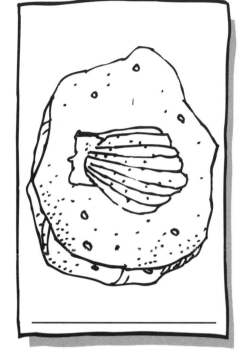

_____

_____

This is how a fossil is made:

_____

_____

_____

_____

_____

_____

_____

Geology • EMC 857

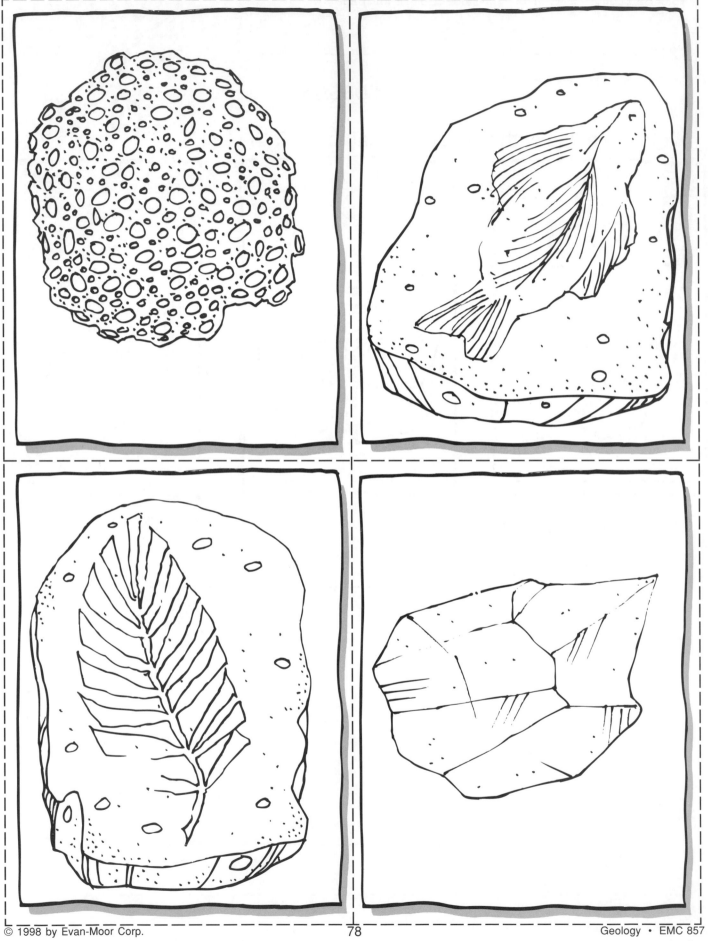

79

ScienceWorks for Kids

Additional Science Resource Books

Big Book Stories & Reproducible Minibooks

Integrate science and reading. Each 11" x 17" book has 8 black & white fully-illustrated stories, each with a reproducible minibook. 64 pp. each. Grades K-2.

How to Do Science Experiments with Children

Teacher instructions and student record sheets for 75 experiments and demonstrations. Concepts include air, sound, water, electricity, light, and chemistry. 240 pp. Grades 1-3. EMC 846

Hands-On Science—Themes for the Whole Year

10 hands-on themes—teacher instructions and reproducible student lab books. Sound, Magnets, Aquarium, Sink & Float, Bubbles & Air, Color, Cold & Heat, Foods, Plants, Mealworms & Snails. 96 pp. Grades 1-3. EMC 828

Science & Math—How to Make Books with Children Series

Create student-authored books on 36 science topics and 14 math topics. Step-by-step directions and reproducible writing forms and patterns. 160 pp. Grades 1-6. EMC 298

How to Write Simple Science Reports

Reproducible forms and illustrations, writing suggestions, discussion starters, and science information. 30 reports in the categories of wild animals, animal homes, and prehistoric animals. 128 pp. Grades 1-4. EMC 395

Big Book of Science Rhymes and Chants

32 rhymes and chants to teach science concepts. Each one is on a separate page with illustrations that are among Evan-Moor's best. 64 pp. Grades K-2. EMC 306

Giant Science Resource Book

It's all in here: picture cards, diagrams, graphic organizers, and student activity sheets; organized by science topics—life science, physical science, earth science, space science, and environmental science. 304 pp. Grades 1-6. EMC 398

Science Picture Cards

24 full-color, 8 1/2" x 11" cards; science information on backs of cards.

EMC 857

Evan-Moor
EDUCATIONAL PUBLISHERS

MPC995

God bless America,

Land that I love,

Stand beside her

And guide her

Through the night with a light from above.

From the mountains,

To the prairies,

To the oceans white with foam,

God bless America,

My home sweet home.

God Bless America

Words and Music by
IRVING BERLIN

While the storm clouds gather ∗ Far across the sea,

Let us swear allegiance ∗ To a land that's free;

Let us all be grateful ∗ For a land so fair,

As we raise our voices ∗ In a solemn prayer.

God   bless   A - mer - i - ca,_____   land

that   I   love._____   Stand be - side   her_____   and

guide   her_____   thru the   night   with a   light   from a - bove._____

"God Bless America" by Irving Berlin was first published in 1938. Almost as soon as the song began generating revenue, Mr. Berlin established the God Bless America Fund to benefit American youth. Most of the earnings from "God Bless America" have been donated to two youth organizations with which Mr. and Mrs. Berlin were personally involved: the Girl Scout Council of Greater New York, and the Greater New York Councils of the Boy Scouts of America. These councils do not discriminate on any basis and are committed to serving all segments of New York City's diverse youth population.

The trustees of the God Bless America Fund are working with the two councils to ensure that funding is allocated for New York City children affected by the tragic events of September 11, 2001.

A portion of the publisher's proceeds is also being donated to the God Bless America Fund.

To the children of New York and
their friends everywhere
—*L.M.*

ISBN 0-439-56213-9

Copyright © 1938, 1939 by Irving Berlin. Text copyright © 1965, 1966 by Irving Berlin. © Copyright Assigned to the Trustees of the God Bless America Fund. International Copyright Secured. Illustrations copyright © 2002 by Lynn Munsinger. All rights reserved. Published by Scholastic Inc., 557 Broadway, New York, NY 10012, by arrangement with HarperCollins Publishers. SCHOLASTIC and associated logos are trademarks and/or registered trademarks of Scholastic Inc.

12 11 10 9 8 7 6 5 4   7 8/0

Printed in the U.S.A.   40

First Scholastic printing, September 2003